The Architecture of the Shakers

The Architecture of the
SHAKERS

JULIE NICOLETTA

PHOTOGRAPHY BY BRET MORGAN

FOREWORD BY ROBERT P. EMLEN

A Norfleet Press Book

The Countryman Press • Woodstock, Vermont

A Norfleet Press Book
New York, New York

Published by The Countryman Press, Inc.
PO Box 175, Woodstock, Vermont 05091

FIRST EDITION

Library of Congress Cataloguing-in-Publication Data

Nicoletta, Julie.
    The architecture of the Shakers / Julie Nicoletta; photography by
Bret Morgan; foreword by Robert P. Emlen.
        p. cm.
    "A Norfleet press book."
    Includes bibliographical references and index.
    ISBN 0-88150-310-X (acid-free paper) : $40.00.
    1. Architecture, Shaker. 1. Morgan, Bret. 11. Title.
NA710.N53   1995
720'.8'8288—dc20   94-23258
                                                    CIP

Director & Producer: John G. Tucker
Designer: Tom Stvan
Editor: Sabra Maya Feldman

1 2 3 4 5 6 7 8 9 10

Printed and bound in China

Frontispiece: Spiral staircases at trustees' office (1839–41), Pleasant Hill, Kentucky.

CONTENTS

CONTENTS

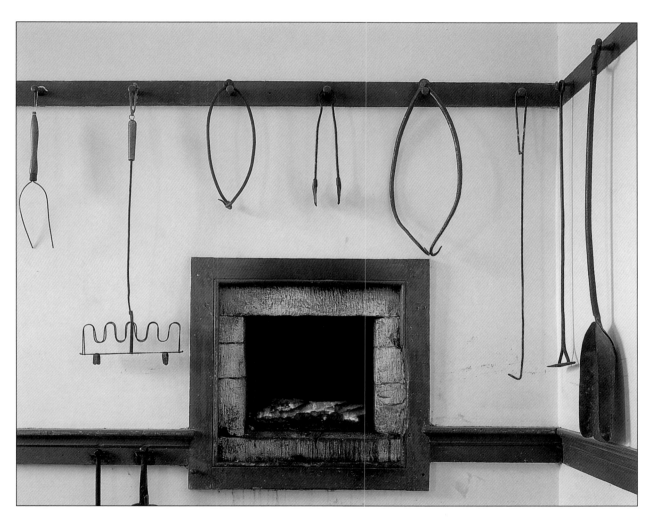

Kitchen, Center Family dwelling house (1824–34), Pleasant Hill, Kentucky.

Foreword

The Distinctiveness of Shaker Architecture

BY ROBERT P. EMLEN

ONE SUMMER DAY YEARS AGO I was driving the back roads of Maine with the guidebook on the dashboard, looking for the Shaker village at Sabbathday Lake. As I passed by the clapboarded frame farmhouses and connected barns of Cumberland County, I wondered if these plain structures might be part of the Shaker village. "Nope," said the woman at a little country store where I stopped to ask the way. "Just up the road. You'll know it when you see it."

I wasn't so sure. What made the storekeeper think I would recognize a place I had never been? Over the years, I had driven many a mile on several continents admiring all sorts of architecture. In graduate school, I had memorized the styles of

These nineteenth-century barns now house sheep raised by the Sabbathday Lake, Maine, Shakers.

American buildings for slide exams. Still, I had no mental image of a Shaker village. I wondered if I might drive right past this one without knowing it. And then, as I came over the hill, flanking the road before me was a compact and tidy village of substantial buildings. Although they generally resembled those I had passed on the farms and in the towns down the road, this place was clearly different. I knew that I had arrived in a Shaker village.

My memories of that first visit to Sabbathday Lake bring to mind the words of nineteenth-century travelers who recorded their initial impressions of Shaker villages. Invariably, their accounts remark on the distinctive appearance of the settlements: the number and quality of the buildings, the neat and clean look of the landscape, the air of prosperity about the community, the sense that Shaker villages are unmistakably different from the homes of their rural neighbors. The broad styles of Shaker architecture are not unique, nor are their building materials, nor their ways of working wood and cutting stone and forging metal. The real difference lies in how Shakers lived their lives—and the homes they made for themselves reflect that distinctiveness.

To begin with, Shakers lived communally, and to this end, they created entire villages large enough to support hundreds of souls joined in a common purpose of work and worship. This unified sense of purpose guided them as they shaped their environment. The Shakers controlled enough land to level hillsides, redirect stream beds, and plow the soil into large, contiguous, even fields. Moreover, they could marshal the labor to do it. Even the biggest and most prosperous farm families of early nineteenth-century America didn't operate on this scale.

The unusual prospect of the Shaker landscape makes just as clear an impression on visitors today as it did over a century ago. Those early visitors marveled at the architecture of individual buildings, often noting design solutions the Shakers devised in response to the requirements of communal living. Dwellings for a hundred of the faithful could be so large—often the biggest buildings in the surrounding countryside—that Shaker craftsmen had to address the problems of the sheer size of their structures. They introduced interior windows, for instance, to carry daylight from exterior walls through rooms and into the darkest corners of the attics. Meetinghouse roofs had to be self-supporting, their interiors uninterrupted by columns or partitions, to allow the unencumbered movement of religious dance. Buildings used jointly by brethren and sisters were designed with

parallel, exclusive facilities—duplicate doorways and duplicate stairways.

Early visitors reported their fascination with innovative storage systems, efficient barns, or cleverly designed laundry facilities. Clearly, the form of Shaker architecture followed the function of life in the spiritual community. Whether or not we have tried to analyze it, most visitors to these villages over the last two centuries have sensed the special quality of Shaker architecture.

The Shakers were seldom victims of fashion. Their buildings bespeak forthright, contemplative lives, freed from the influences of the outside world. Stylistic considerations were not high on the list of Shaker priorities; to the contrary, buildings were designed to outlast the vagaries of changing tastes. They had to be efficient, easy to maintain, and give their builders a sense of serenity and grace from knowing that what they created was as close to perfection as humanly possible.

Nineteenth-century visitors wrote of the unity of design in Shaker villages. Developed according to the community's standards and requirements, the buildings in a Shaker village are more consistent in appearance than those of the neighboring farms. Their clustering on the land, the way they relate to one another in function and scale, the consistency of aesthetic choices employed by Shaker craftsmen, all attest to that communal society of spiritual brethren and sisters devoted to creating an ideal life on earth.

This way of life distinguishes Shaker architecture from the architecture of other communal villages. Nowhere is this difference more obvious than in the present appearance of former Shaker villages adapted in the twentieth century as resorts, prisons, nursing homes, and seminaries. Although they still support communal living, these villages have been modified to serve needs unknown to the Shakers. One finds there only the vestiges of Shaker architecture.

The appearance of the village at Sabbathday Lake must have been distinctive in the mind of the storekeeper. It was settled by the Shakers in 1794 and has been home to the community for more than two hundred years. Small wonder I could recognize those buildings at first sight.

At Sabbathday Lake, the meeting house (1794) overlooks the brick dwelling house (1883).

Introduction

THIS BOOK PRESENTS Shaker architecture as the Shakers conceived it, built it, and used it. Through original research, new color photographs, and historic images, Shaker architecture is revealed as more than a mute memorial to a communal society that has lasted over two hundred years. Shaker society was and is complex; the sect's architecture reflects this complexity. Thus, this book will argue that the buildings should not be seen merely as the simple architecture of a simple people. Instead, the buildings are presented as living structures that changed over time as the Shakers' lives and needs changed.

Buildings at all the Shaker communities, from Maine to Kentucky, and of each building type, from meeting houses to workshops, dwelling houses to

Center Family dwelling house (1824–34), Pleasant Hill, Kentucky.

barns, are discussed. Within this framework, the design, construction, building materials, and function of Shaker structures can be explored as components of a society that struggled to create a kingdom of heaven on earth. Through the buildings we see successes and failures, the physical remnants of a social experiment that flourished in the early nineteenth century only to slowly decline from the second half of the last century until the present.

Ironically, this decline has encouraged the popularity of Shaker objects among collectors, designers, and, most recently, a wider public. In the twentieth century, Shaker architecture, furniture, and crafts not only became collectable, but have also had a strong impact on modern design. The clean lines of Shaker exteriors and interiors and their similarity to the large, solemn structures of factories and grain elevators captured the imagination of the artist Charles Sheeler, who photographed and painted Shaker images in the 1930s and 1940s. The Index of American Design, a 1930s project of the National Gallery of Art which documented objects and architecture from America's past and included numerous Shaker objects and buildings, helped to spread the concept of "Shaker style"—a notion alien to the Shakers themselves. The Shaker legacy of plain wood forms anticipated twentieth-century works by Frank Lloyd Wright, Le Corbusier, Mies van der Rohe, and others.

In recent years, Shaker forms have become popular not only through reproductions by highly skilled craftspeople, but also through less expensive, mass-produced interpretations. This latest wave of commercialization has threatened to reduce the Shakers' physical heritage to mere token objects without acknowledging the religious meaning and social experimentation that created these works in the first place. It is hoped that this book will illuminate the significance of architecture in the Shaker experience, as well as its impact on mainstream culture.

Porch, Enfield House (1826; moved 1918), Canterbury, New Hampshire. This porch is a late-nineteenth-century addition to the dwelling house.

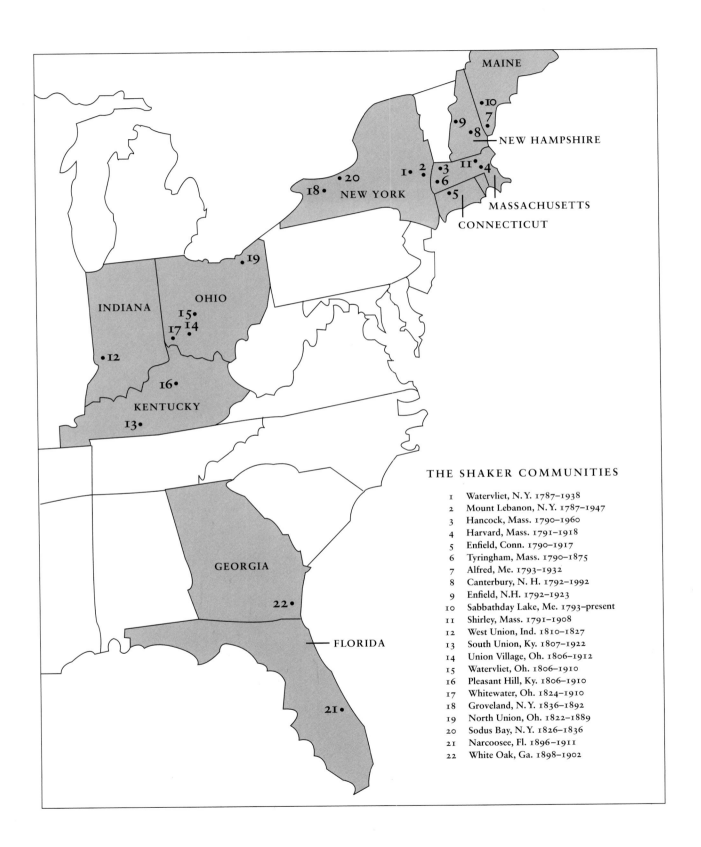

MAINE

•10
7
•9
•8
NEW HAMPSHIRE

1• 2• •3 11•• 4
•6
18• •5
NEW YORK MASSACHUSETTS

CONNECTICUT

•19

INDIANA OHIO

15•
17• 14•

•12

16•

KENTUCKY

13•

GEORGIA

22•

FLORIDA

21•

THE SHAKER COMMUNITIES

1	Watervliet, N.Y. 1787–1938
2	Mount Lebanon, N.Y. 1787–1947
3	Hancock, Mass. 1790–1960
4	Harvard, Mass. 1791–1918
5	Enfield, Conn. 1790–1917
6	Tyringham, Mass. 1790–1875
7	Alfred, Me. 1793–1932
8	Canterbury, N. H. 1792–1992
9	Enfield, N.H. 1792–1923
10	Sabbathday Lake, Me. 1793–present
11	Shirley, Mass. 1791–1908
12	West Union, Ind. 1810–1827
13	South Union, Ky. 1807–1922
14	Union Village, Oh. 1806–1912
15	Watervliet, Oh. 1806–1910
16	Pleasant Hill, Ky. 1806–1910
17	Whitewater, Oh. 1824–1910
18	Groveland, N.Y. 1836–1892
19	North Union, Oh. 1822–1889
20	Sodus Bay, N.Y. 1826–1836
21	Narcoosee, Fl. 1896–1911
22	White Oak, Ga. 1898–1902

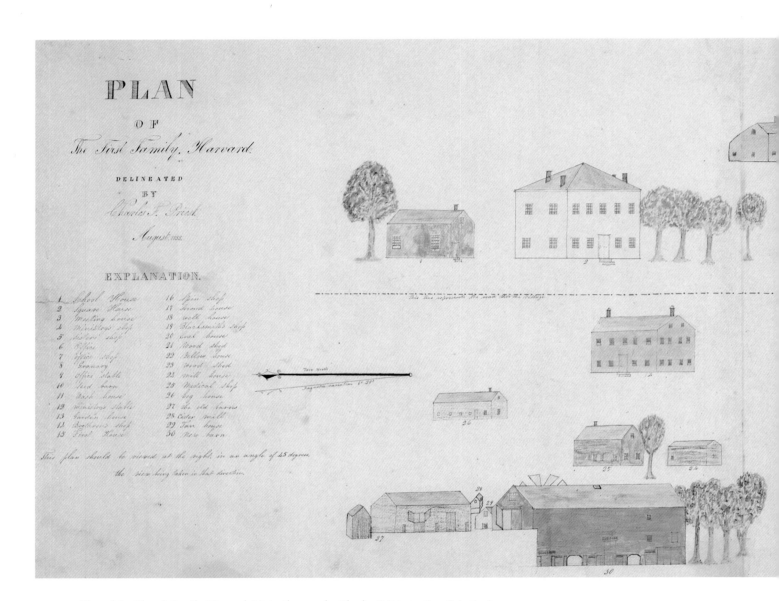

Plan of the Church Family, Harvard, Massachusetts, by Charles F. Priest, 1833. Priest's view of Harvard depicts the 1769 Square House in the upper left. It also reveals the Shakers' use of gambrel roofs on dwelling houses in the early part of the nineteenth century. (Collection of the Library of Congress, Geography and Maps Division.)

1 Shaker Communities

The Establishment of Shakerism in America

IN 1774 A BAND OF EIGHT SHAKERS arrived in New York City after a two-month journey that began in Manchester, England. Led by Mother Ann Lee, the sect had been driven from England by persecution stemming from Ann Lee's assertion that she embodied the Christ spirit—a sign, she claimed, that the Millennium was at hand. Lee had joined a radical religious group called the Shaking Quakers sometime in the late 1760s or early 1770s, gaining a leadership role by 1772. In New York, the Shakers, officially known as the United Society of Believers in Christ's Second Appearing, gradually made their way to a place called Niskeyuna (now known as Watervliet) just northwest of Albany. By this time Lee's husband, who accompanied her to New York, had left her. But the group gained a few members. They purchased a small parcel of land there in 1776 and set about establishing a community based on religious devotion, celibacy, and communal labor.

Encouraged by religious revivalism in the countryside, the Shakers launched a two-year missionary trip across eastern New York and New England, gathering many converts. The Shakers found their greatest success in rural areas where the fires of revivalism burned the brightest. The northeastern countryside, undergoing economic change as industrialization slowly progressed, spawned numerous religious revivals from the mid-eighteenth century to the early nineteenth century. For many individuals, the Shakers offered a form of worship that provided an immediacy of feeling and satisfaction not found in more established religions, such as Congregationalism. Lee and her

1-1   This view looks south to the Canterbury, New Hampshire, Shaker village, with the stone foundation of the Church Family's cow barn in the foreground.

companions often stayed for several months in the homes of recent converts, enabling them to establish small Shaker communities by the time the missionaries moved on to the next town. However, the Shakers' success provoked the hostility of established religious leaders and rural inhabitants who viewed the Shakers as a threat to traditional society. Despite numerous setbacks (including the imprisonment of Ann Lee on the accusation that she was a British spy during the Revolutionary War), the sect continued to grow, establishing communities throughout the Northeast. By the time of Ann Lee's death in 1784, the Shakers were a loosely organized society of more than ten settlements with several hundred members.

After her death, Ann Lee became a mythical figure in Shakerism (figure 1-2). At certain periods she played a major role in intense religious revivals, such as "Mother Ann's Work," which lasted from 1837 to 1845. Mother Ann also had an influence through Shaker publications issued in the early nineteenth century, most significantly in the *Testimonies of the Life, Character, Revelations and Doctrines of Our Ever Blessed Mother Ann Lee, and the Elders With Her.* This work attributed sayings to her concerning Shaker attitudes toward labor and perfection such as, "Do all your work as though you had a thousand years to live, and as you would if you knew you must die tomorrow."[1]

Gathering into Gospel Order

Joseph Meacham, one of Ann Lee's successors, played the major role in transforming Shakerism into an organized religion by setting down rules for worship, communal property, social behavior, and architecture. Whereas Ann Lee had emphasized the individual and emotional aspects of religious expression, Meacham saw spiritual salvation as attainable through discipline in all parts of life. Architecture played a major role by helping to establish hierarchies of members and providing specialized spaces for temporal and spiritual activities. In 1787 Meacham established the first official Shaker community by "gathering" the Believers at Mount Lebanon, New York, where he had first

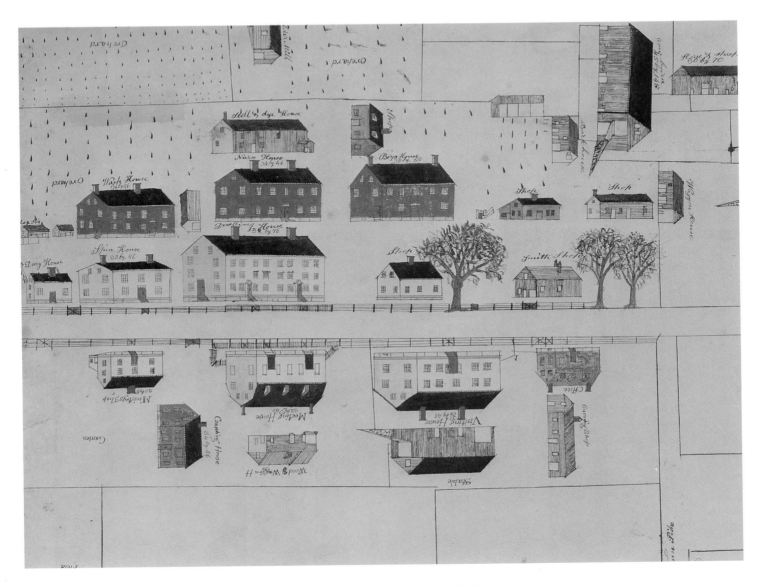

1-3   Plan of Alfred, Maine, by Joshua Bussell, 1845. This detail of the Church Family shows that despite laws demanding that only the meeting house be painted white, the Shakers painted other buildings white as well. Secondary structures like shops, however, were painted red. (Collection of the Library of Congress, Geography and Maps Division.)

1-2   (opposite) In 1835 the Shakers exhumed Mother Ann Lee's remains from her original grave and moved them to their present location in the Shaker cemetery at Watervliet, New York. The marker was placed on the grave sometime in the nineteenth century.

joined the Shakers. This settlement, originally called New Lebanon, became known as Mount Lebanon in the mid-nineteenth century to differentiate the Shaker village from the nearby town of New Lebanon. As the site where Meacham made his decisions and formed his ministry, Mount Lebanon quickly became the head Shaker commu-

nity, serving in this capacity until its closure in 1947. By 1794 eleven villages, including Mount Lebanon, were established in "gospel order," that is, they officially became communal societies with shared property and shared duties. These villages were: Watervliet, New York, 1787; Hancock and Tyringham, Massachusetts, and Enfield,

Connecticut, 1790; Harvard and Shirley, Massachusetts, 1791; Canterbury and Enfield, New Hampshire, 1792; and Alfred and Sabbathday Lake (then known as New Gloucester), Maine, 1793 (figures 1-1 and 1-3).

Meacham established the separate but equal nature of the sexes, stating that "the man & the woman have Equal Rights in order & Lots & in the Lead & Government of the Church according to their Sex in this Latter Day."[2] Thus, brothers and sisters held equal roles of leadership at the various levels of Shaker life. In addition, Meacham separated each community into "families" organized along spiritual rather than blood lines because he believed that converts had to break all natural familial ties to commit themselves fully to Christ. Shaker families provided a sense of identity to fill the void left by the giving up of one's own relatives. The First Family, which later became known as the Church Family in the East and the Center Family in the West, functioned as the core of each Shaker village (figure 1-4). The members of this family were those who devoted themselves body and soul to Shakerism by signing the Covenant, a legal document in which a Shaker gave all his or her worldly possessions to the community. Each family had its own set of buildings, but the meeting house stood on the property of the First Family. Other families were formed in relation to the Church Family, often taking names based on their geographical locations. Thus, the North Family stood to the north of the Church Family, the South Family to the south. In most villages, the North Family functioned as the "gathering order," where an individual who had just entered the community could learn more about the ways of the sect. Sometimes smaller families became known by the buildings they lived in or by the goods they produced. Union Village, Ohio, included the East House Family, the West Frame House Family, and the Grist Mill Family.

Not only did the families provide spiritual support for a brother or sister, but they also defined an individual's place in the community. The Church Family consisted of the purest members of Shakerism, who risked being tainted through contact with members of other families. The Millennial Laws of 1821 (based on Ann Lee and Joseph Meacham's rules guiding all aspects of Shaker life and expanded by later Shaker leaders) stated that members of different families were not allowed to interact unless the elders permitted it. This rule attempted to prevent the possibility of spiritual or physical contamination among families that were not equal in terms of spiritual perfection. The separate family areas with their own dwelling houses, shops, and barns, emphasized this isolation by shaping each family's physical space. Nevertheless, Shaker records indicate that members of different families often did meet in worship, work, and recreation without penalty. Eventually, economic status outweighed spiritual hierarchy. For example, in the nineteenth century Mount Lebanon's South Family assumed a greater leadership role by virtue of its success in producing and marketing Shaker chairs.

1-4 A view of the Center Family from the East Family cooper's shop (foreground; moved 1847), Pleasant Hill, Kentucky. In the background are the Center Family dwelling house (1824–34), the water house (1833), and the brethren's bath house (1860).

Growth of Eastern Communities

All the eastern communities grew quickly in the late eighteenth and early nineteenth centuries, fired by continued religious revivals in rural areas where the Shakers settled. Because of the centralized control exerted by Meacham and his successors at Mount Lebanon, Shaker villages in the Northeast came to resemble one another architecturally. Circulation of the Millennial Laws, through letters and visits, helped define common architectural forms in the early nineteenth century. Although the extent to which the Laws were actually followed is still unknown, the arrangement of buildings (such as meeting houses and dwelling houses), and the colors of buildings (such as meeting houses and barns), indicate that the Shakers at different villages followed many of the rules pertaining to their physical environment. Another unifying factor among villages was the scale of communal organization, which required specialized structures to accommodate specific functions. Thus, each village had a meeting house, dwelling houses, barns, workshops, and various outbuildings. As the communities grew, labor became increasingly specialized, creating a need for tan houses, broom shops, cooper shops, and spinning shops. Shaker communities created an identity recognizable in their tidy yards and roads and in their clusters of large, spare build-

1-6 The cove cornice on the Church Family dwelling (1875–77) at Mount Lebanon, New York, appears on other Shaker structures at the village as well as at Watervliet, New York, and Hancock, Massachusetts. Belfries topped most Shaker dwellings. The bells marked times for rising, retiring, and eating meals.

1-5 The Shaker builder Micajah Burnett used raised mortar as both a decorative and functional device, as seen on the Center Family dwelling house (1824–34) at Pleasant Hill. The mortar adds texture to the facade of the building and helps the stone shed water.

ings set in the countryside. Here, the Shakers produced goods for their own use and for sale to the outside world.

Despite their large size and diverse economies, Shaker villages were never entirely self-sufficient; they depended on trade with the world, a dependency that increased as the years passed. These communities, both agricultural and industrial, represented in microcosm the industrialization of American society—a society that shifted from a largely agricultural one based on hand tools and manual labor to a largely industrial one based on machinery and mass production.

Establishment of Shakerism in the West

After nearly twenty years of establishing settlements and refining the doctrine of Shakerism, the elders and eldresses at Mount Lebanon, led by Joseph Meacham's female counterpart and successor, Lucy Wright, decided to expand their religion westward. Hearing of religious revivals in Cane Ridge, Kentucky, the Shakers sent three brothers on foot to spread the word in early 1805. As in New England, the Shakers met with great success in gathering converts not only in Kentucky but also in Ohio. This success brought persecution, again from local ministers and settlers who saw the Shakers as a threat to the solidity of their congregations and communities. Nevertheless, the Shakers established many villages in the following years: Union Village and Watervliet, Ohio, and Pleasant Hill, Kentucky, 1806; South Union, Kentucky, 1807; North Union, Ohio, 1822; and Whitewater, Ohio, 1824. The westernmost Shaker village, West Union, Indiana, was short-lived. Established in 1810 in a swampy area of western Indiana, it suffered from outbreaks of malaria as well as from skirmishes with Native Americans. The Shakers abandoned it in 1827 and no buildings remain. The surviving members joined the community at Whitewater. Despite difficulties such as those at West Union, the Shakers were a strong presence in the United States, with nineteen permanent communities founded by 1826.

Short-lived Communities

The Shakers formed three other short-term communities in the East in the early nineteenth century. Gorham, Maine (1808-19), and Savoy, Massachusetts (1817–25), were both small villages established by groups of Believers who already lived there before their conversions. Since the villages never expanded in size, the ministry elders overseeing the two communities decided to move the Gorham Shakers to Sabbathday Lake in 1819 and the Savoy Shakers to Mount Lebanon and Watervliet, New York, in 1825. By the early nineteenth century, Shaker villages required hundreds of members to remain economically viable. A third community, Sodus Bay, New York (1826-36), was situated on the shore of Lake Ontario. Although this settlement flourished both agriculturally (due to the rich soil) and commercially (due to its waterfront location), the Shakers were forced to abandon the site when the state of New York granted permission for the construction of the Sodus Canal through their property. The Sodus Bay Shakers established a new community at Groveland, New York (near Rochester), from 1836 to 1838, remaining there until 1892, when the ministry closed the village.

The Believers established three other short-lived communities in other parts of the country in the nineteenth century. A small group of Shaker sisters, mostly African-American, lived together in a row house in Philadelphia. Under the direction of

1-7 The East Family dwelling house (1817) at Pleasant Hill has a symmetrical facade with numerous windows—a typical feature of both eastern and western dwellings.

Mother Rebecca Jackson, an African-American woman who converted to Shakerism in 1846, the sisters supported themselves by taking in laundry and working as maids in worldly homes. Following the death of Mother Rebecca in 1871, the community slowly died out. In the 1890s, the Shakers established two small communities in the South in Narcoosee, Florida (1896-1911), and White Oak, Georgia (1898-1902). They hoped to find converts in the area as well as to provide a comfortable place for elderly Shakers to live. The Shakers there lived in existing structures, except for a large dwelling house at White Oak, which they had built for them in 1899. Despite the money and effort poured into the communities, the missionary movement was unsuccessful because the Shakers in the South could not support themselves. Narcoosee and White Oak's distance from the other Shaker settlements and their expensive maintenance forced the villages' closings in the early twentieth century.

Growth of Western Communities

The western Shaker villages represented a somewhat different form of Shakerism. Geographically distant from the central ministry of Mount Lebanon, the western Shakers only loosely adhered to the Millennial Laws, changing the rules to meet their own needs and their more worldly way of life. The product of a later missionary effort, the western Shakers never had direct contact with the sect's founder, Mother Ann, or her immediate successors. The historian Stephen J. Stein has noted that the correspondence between the East and the West and the religious publications of the two groups reveal theological differences, tensions,

and personality conflicts.[3] Brothers in the western communities issued the first published works setting down the doctrines of Shaker theology. By doing so, they created an intellectual core at Union Village and Pleasant Hill that threatened to undermine the leadership of Mount Lebanon. The leaders in the West were also less conservative than those in the East, and thus were "more willing to celebrate the emergence of republicanism" in the United States.[4] This strong streak of individualism fostered a lifestyle that was more connected to the outside world and less disciplined than that of the eastern Shakers.

Regional Differences in Shaker Architecture

Regional differences can be seen to some extent in the buildings of the western communities. Although Shaker leaders in the East sought architectural standardization, Shaker buildings varied from East to West. As in the East, the buildings of the western villages relied on local materials and regional forms. Many western villages used log houses for dwellings, kitchens, and workshops well into the 1830s. Although some early buildings were wood frame, the Kentucky Shakers favored structures of brick and limestone, materials they claimed were more readily available than wood (figures 1-5 and 1-7). The structures the western Shakers built often display an appreciation for worldly ornament—such as beading and other moldings—not allowed under the Millennial Laws, which forbade any type of decoration as superfluous. Also, because of the southern climate, the Shakers, like their non-Shaker neighbors, constructed buildings

1-8 Curved brackets support a gabled roof above the entrance to the ministry shop (1848) at Canterbury, New Hampshire. These door hoods, added in the mid-nineteenth century, are typical features of the Canterbury Church Family.

with high ceilings, large windows, and wide hallways to facilitate air circulation. Despite these differences, the western Shaker villages largely followed the patterns of settlement established in the East: large, neatly kept structures arranged along the main roads that ran through the villages.

In addition to architectural differences between East and West, Shaker buildings often varied from one community to another both in general form and detail. At the communities of Watervliet and Mount Lebanon, New York, and Hancock, Massachusetts, many buildings had cove cornices (figure

1-6). These are wide concave moldings running between the roof overhang and the exterior walls. These moldings were not a Shaker invention; they can be found on early eighteenth-century houses in the Boston area. The shed roofs protecting many entrance doors on eastern buildings had their precedents in eighteenth-century houses built by English and Dutch settlers in the Hudson River valley. Canterbury, New Hampshire, later developed its own gabled entrance roofs supported by curved brackets (figure 1-8). Many buildings in the western communities had rear kitchen wings, called "ells," and single front entrances covered by semi-circular fanlights, rather than separate entrances for men and women as in the East (figures 1-9 and 1-10).

These differences reveal a continuity with building traditions originating outside Shakerdom. The presence of such details indicates that Shaker buildings were not as simple in appearance as many historians have argued. Indeed, the elders allowed some decoration, even in the East in the early years, because it was part of a language of building familiar to the largely New England-born membership. Often having learned carpentry and joinery before entering the sect, Shaker builders built what they knew.

Another long-held myth is that the Shakers built all their buildings with their own labor. An examination of written records shows that even in the early years of the society, the Shakers often hired non-Shakers for building projects. Sometimes these hired builders merely assisted the Shakers, other times they designed and erected structures in their entirety. The Shakers were often hindered by a shortage of labor. In the early years, so many buildings were constructed at the same time that the communities could not simultaneously build and perform all the daily tasks required without hiring extra hands. Later in the nineteenth century, the decline in the number of able-bodied male Shakers forced the society to look to the world to fill not only building but also farming and manufacturing jobs. In his history of the Church Family at Mount Lebanon, written in 1856, Isaac N. Youngs notes the problems entailed by hiring outsiders to perform work, particularly the introduction of worldly influences on the Shakers. He fervently hoped that the Shakers would become more self-sufficient, but instead they became increasingly dependent on the outside world.[5]

Community Planning

Although the Shakers established rules concerning the maintenance and cleanliness of their villages, they did not have specific laws determining how a community should be laid out. Because the Shakers drew converts primarily from rural areas, villages developed on farm land. In nearly every case, the Shaker community developed on and around the first parcel of land donated by an early convert. Usually this land already had some buildings on it and had been cultivated to some extent. In addition, this property often abutted a major road. As Shaker villages expanded they eventually straddled highways and trade routes. Both Hancock and Mount Lebanon, for instance, stand along the road that became Route 20, running from Boston to Buffalo. In the twentieth century, the state of New York moved Route 20 to bypass the village of Mount Lebanon, leaving the site hidden from the main road today. In Ohio, Union Village stood at the crossroads of highways running to Lebanon, Dayton, and Cincinnati.

From 1837 to 1839 the Shakers at Pleasant Hill, under the supervision of Micajah Burnett, the community's builder, constructed the section of the main turnpike between Harrodsburg and Lexington that ran through the center of their village. The Shakers participated in the construction as a means of controlling traffic on the road while still profiting from it. Not only did Pleasant Hill stand along an important road, but it also managed ferry traffic across the Kentucky River at a point near the village.

1-9   Pleasant Hill's Center Family dwelling (1824–34), with its long three-story ell, demonstrates the great size of Shaker houses in the western communities.

1-10 The wide fanlight spanning the front entrance of the trustees' office (1839–41) at Pleasant Hill was inspired by worldly architectural features of the early nineteenth century.

In general, the Shakers placed their most important buildings along these main roads and located secondary buildings behind the main ones. Canterbury, New Hampshire, and Watervliet, New York, are exceptions to this rule. Although the Canterbury Church Family buildings flank both sides of the main road, dominant structures, such as the meeting house and the dwelling house, stand off to the east along granite walkways. Other buildings are also arranged in rows running perpendicular to the main road (figure 1-1, page 18). The location of the early Shaker buildings at Canterbury was determined largely by the presence of pre-Shaker buildings erected by Benjamin Whitcher, whose land formed the core of the Shaker community there after his conversion.

The community at Watervliet, New York, developed in a different way. The Shakers purchased a tract of unimproved swampland in 1776. They drained the land, cultivated fields, and laid out the different families as units set off from the main road (connecting Albany and Schenectady). The Church Family developed around a road running perpendicular to the main road, thus forming a sort of village green with the family's first dwelling house at the top of the road and the meeting house, workshops, and office on either side of the road. The other families at Watervliet also developed in groups set off from the main road around their own large open spaces.

The Shakers shaped their landscapes by constructing buildings, roads, ramps, dams, ponds, and waterworks. Despite this constant reworking of the land, they were equally resourceful in adapting themselves to their surroundings. In hilly areas, such as eastern New York and New England, the Shakers often built their buildings into the sides of slopes so that entrances provided access at different levels. This practice can be seen in nearly every kind of building from dwellings to barns.

Shaker communities, whether eastern or western, can be seen as the physical embodiment of the beliefs and practices of the communal society. Celibacy, division of labor, worship—all these elements of Shaker life were represented in the buildings themselves and in their relationships with each other. The various building types were components of a scheme that not only established order but also used the villages as advertisements of Shakerism to visitors from the outside world. The Shakers hoped that through the prosperity and orderliness of their villages they would create a better society.

At the peak of Shakerism, around 1840, the sect numbered over 3600 members.[6] The larger villages were huge settlements encompassing thousands of acres of land and several hundred members. Smaller villages had approximately forty to one hundred members. In addition to the celibate families, many villages also encompassed several "out families," nuclear families interested in Shakerism. These groups lived apart from the main body of Believers, but were welcome to join the community more fully if they wished. In this way the Shakers controlled the environments surrounding their village cores.

When visiting a Shaker village today, one must keep in mind that the remains of a site represent only a fraction of the buildings that once stood. In most cases, only the structures of one family, usually the Church or Center Family, remain. Buildings of additional families still stand at some villages, such as Mount Lebanon or Pleasant Hill, providing a better sense of the size and density of Shaker settlements.

2 Meeting Houses

The Standardization of Worship

THE CONSTRUCTION OF THE FIRST Shaker meeting houses in the 1780s marked the advent of Shaker architecture. These buildings not only performed the practical function of providing a place of worship for an entire Shaker village, they also symbolized a shift in worship practices. In addition, their standardization of form throughout the New York and New England communities began to define the appearance of the villages and create a sense of identity among the Believers themselves.

2-1 The Sabbathday Lake, Maine, meeting house (1794), in use for two hundred years, is one of three early Shaker meeting houses that retains its original appearance. The other two can be found at Canterbury, New Hampshire (figure 2-11), and Hancock, Massachusetts, the latter originally built in 1792–93 at the Shaker village in Shirley, Massachusetts, and moved to Hancock in 1962. Mount Lebanon, New York's first meeting house (1786–87) still stands, though in a different form. The Shakers raised its gambrel roof after 1839 to use the building as a seed shop.

Early Meeting Houses

The Shakers built their first meeting house at Mount Lebanon from 1786 to 1787. Under the guidance of James Whittaker and Joseph Meacham and relying on the carpentry and joinery skills of Moses Johnson, the Shakers erected a small, approximately 44-by-32-foot, timber-frame structure 2½ stories tall (figure 2-1). The building resembled the Anglo-Dutch architecture of the Hudson River valley, Long Island, and the southern shore of Connecticut. This architecture combined elements of English and Dutch building forms, particularly English gambrel roofs and the exposed, closely spaced beams and knee braces common in Dutch building (figure 2-2). These features can be seen in all the Shakers' early meeting houses. By borrowing these architectural forms, the Shakers created a structure that left the first floor, the main meeting room, an open space. In addition, they altered this building type by including two separate front entrance doors (figure 2-11, page 46). These doors, the left for the brothers and the right for the sisters, represented the celibate but largely equal relationship of the sexes within Shakerism. A third door on the side provided separate access for the ministry.

The presence of unimpeded space was crucial in Shaker worship because dances were an integral part of the religious meeting. Whereas the Shakers under Mother Ann had worshipped outdoors in woods or fields or in the homes of converts, Meacham brought worship into a single, sacred space. He further defined worship practices by choreographing dances that required coordination of movement rather than the frenzied free shaking and whirling that Ann Lee had encouraged. Shaker families practiced these dances in their own dwellings during the week so they could perform them flawlessly in the public Sunday meetings in the village's meeting house. These meetings lasted most of the day, beginning in the morning, and included a sermon by one of the elders. Shaker dancing exhibited a unity of movement and purpose that was intended to educate and impress visitors from the outside world as well as confirm the participants' own sense of community.

Meacham also encouraged physical perfection through square forms and straight lines. Building within "church order" meant that walls should meet at right angles and have square or rectangular plans. Paths were laid at right angles so that members would not take diagonal shortcuts across door yards. A dance called the "Square Order Shuffle" emphasized the order embodied in the square.

Standardization of Society

Meacham's program of standardization, marked by the erection of Mount Lebanon's meeting house, also applied to the Shaker body. Through standardized dances, hymns, dress, and behavior, the Shakers embraced an ideal of simplicity and saintliness in contrast to the ways of the outside world. Adhering to rules (such as always stepping first with the right foot and remaining silent during meals) kept members constantly aware of the need to fight the natural inclinations of the body, which the Shakers considered an impediment to attaining perfection. By requiring strong self-discipline, Shaker elders hoped to ensure individual subordination to the larger community, which would help create a Shaker identity. A further example of self-discipline concerned educating brothers and sisters to speak differently from people of the world in terms of cadence and vocabulary. One Shaker journal in the collection of the New York Public Library contains an entry for November 1808 that states: "Labers [sic] made to have the Believers correct their awkward habits, particularly in their manner of speaking. So meet on Nov 1 in evening, & couple times a week to practice proper speaking . . ."[7]

The meeting houses were further sanctified by functioning as the homes of the ministry elders and eldresses. Under the Millennial Laws concerning "The Order Office and Calling of The Ministry," the following rule states that:

7. The Ministry may in no wise blend in common with the rest of the people; they may not work under the same roof, live in the same house, nor eat at the same table. But their

2-2 The meeting room of the Sabbathday Lake, Maine, meeting house shows the influence of Anglo-Dutch architecture—transmitted via Mount Lebanon—with closely spaced horizontal beams which support the floor above. These beams allowed an open room for dancing, while large windows flooded the worship area with light.

dwelling place shall be in the meeting house, even in the most holy Sanctuary.[8]

These two men and two women functioned as the leaders of a Shaker bishopric comprising two to three Shaker villages. For example, the Mount Lebanon bishopric encompassed Mount Lebanon and Watervliet, New York. The ministry spent six months living in the meeting house at Mount Lebanon and six months in the meeting house at Watervliet. As the spiritual leaders of the community, they lived in the upper floors of the meeting house, apart from the other brothers and sisters (figure 2-3). Their isolation protected them from

pollution by more worldly people, including other Shakers. In fact, they rarely worshipped with the Shaker families in the meeting house, instead observing the meetings from small interior windows that looked out over the main room of the building (figure 2-4). However, they did meet often with family elders in their own villages and during frequent trips that they took to other Shaker communities. The ministry also enacted various rules on issues ranging from buildings to social behavior in an attempt to control every aspect of Shaker life.

The success of Mount Lebanon's meeting house encouraged the construction of meeting houses at other Shaker villages in the Northeast. From

2-3   Ministry room, meeting house, Sabbathday Lake. The ministry elders and eldresses, representatives of the sect's spiritual leadership, lived on the second floor of the meeting house.

1786 to 1794, Johnson helped build nine more meeting houses: Hancock, Massachusetts (1786); Watervliet, New York (1791); Enfield, Connecticut (1791); Harvard, Massachusetts (1791); Canterbury, New Hampshire (1792–93); Shirley, Massachusetts (1792-93); Enfield, New Hampshire (1793); Sabbathday Lake, Maine (1794); and Alfred, Maine (1794). Johnson, who seems to have been trained as a builder before he converted to Shakerism, traveled from one village to another, staying long enough to supervise the laying of the foundation and the raising of the frame. Thus, all the early meeting houses were nearly identical in size and appearance. In the earliest eastern communities such as Mount Lebanon, these buildings were the first, or among the first, Shaker-built structures.

Meeting houses stood in the physical center of the community as the central place of religious worship, even though families had their daily meetings in their own dwelling houses. Color also set the meeting houses apart from the other buildings in the village. Two rules in the Millennial Laws under "Concerning Building, Painting, Varnishing and the Manufacture of Articles for Sale, &c. &c." specifically refer to meeting houses:

> 3. The meeting house should be painted white without, and of a blueish shade within.

> 6. No buildings may be painted white, save meeting houses.[9]

Although early meeting houses were painted in accordance with the Laws, the Shakers also painted profane buildings white, particularly later in the nineteenth century, as rules in the communities

2-4 Although Pleasant Hill, Kentucky's meeting house (1820) did not take the same exterior form as the earlier New York and New England meeting houses, the Prussian blue paint and pegboards running along the wall recall the eastern buildings of Moses Johnson. The small window in the right-hand corner of the photo allowed the elders and eldresses to observe the worship meetings from their quarters.

became more lax. Of the ten early meeting houses built, only three remain in their original form at the following sites: Hancock Shaker Village (actually the Shirley, Massachusetts, meeting house, moved to Hancock in 1962), Canterbury, New Hampshire, and Sabbathday Lake, Maine. Visitors may still see the Prussian-blue trim on the interior beams and moldings and the yellow-ocher stained floors. The meeting house at Sabbathday Lake continues to be used for Sunday services by the Shaker community living there.

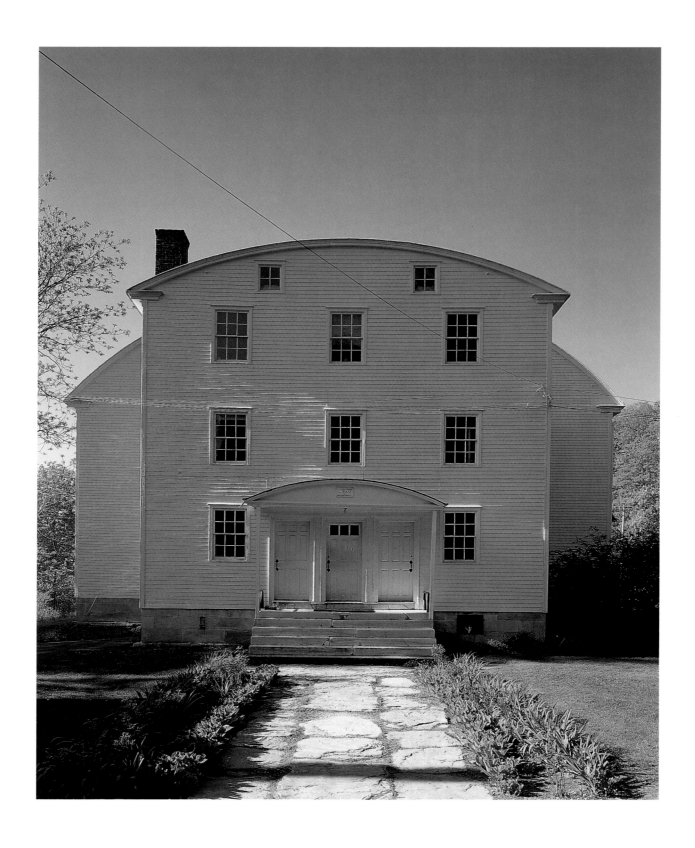

Nineteenth-Century Meeting Houses

Many of the other meeting houses were altered or demolished in subsequent years, sometimes by the Shakers themselves. When the Mount Lebanon Shakers erected a new meeting house in 1824, they moved the old meeting house down the road and used it as a school house until 1839, when they built a new school house. After this date, they raised the structure's gambrel roof to a gable roof and converted the building into a seed shop. At Watervliet, New York, the old meeting house remained standing next to the new one, built in 1847, but the Shakers used it for nonreligious purposes. It was demolished in 1927 after the Church Family buildings had been sold to Albany County. Once a meeting house had fulfilled its original function, the practical-minded Shakers had no qualms about employing the structure or its materials for other purposes.

In some instances villages like Mount Lebanon found that the growing size of their populations required a larger structure to house all the worshippers. Mount Lebanon's new meeting house (1824) is different from any other Shaker structure, though its curved ceiling has precedents in some of the barrel-vaulted churches built in New England in the late eighteenth and early nineteenth centuries (figure 2-5). Designed by a team of brothers of the Church Family, the building, a tour de force of framing and vaulting, features a curved

2-6 The interior of the Mount Lebanon meeting house provided ample room for worship meetings as well as seating for visitors from the world. This photo was taken by N.E. Baldwin in June 1938 when the community was still a Shaker village. The Darrow School altered the interior in the 1960s to accommodate a library. (Historic American Buildings Survey, Collection of the Library of Congress, Prints and Photographs Division.)

roof spanning a space 80 by 65 feet (figure 2-6). Rafters radiating vertically and horizontally from the frame, like spokes in a wheel, support the arched roof and keep the exterior walls from buckling outward. Solid brick piers evenly spaced about three feet apart support the floor of the meeting room, providing a strong foundation to withstand the pounding of stomping feet during Shaker dances. Three doors on the south end of the building provide separate entrances for the brothers, ministry, and sisters. The two doors on the east side allowed male and female visitors to enter through separate doors, too. The expense of the structure and the labor required to build it prohibited its replication at other villages. The unique grandeur of this new meeting house with its curved roof proclaimed the Mount Lebanon ministry's

2-5 The curved roof of the second meeting house (1824) at Mount Lebanon, New York, the lead Shaker village, gives the structure a unique form. The building was the largest meeting house in Shakerdom.

2-7 Designed by Micajah Burnett, the meeting house (1820) at Pleasant Hill, Kentucky, looks back to the symmetry of earlier meeting houses, despite its western gable roof.

power and primacy over the other villages, particularly those in the West.

The meeting houses of the western villages bespeak the differing views and practices of these Shakers. Although all the meeting houses erected in the East were built of wood, meeting houses in the West were constructed of either wood or brick. Copies of lost maps drawn by Brother Isaac N. Youngs on a visit from Mount Lebanon to the western villages in 1834 show all the meeting houses with gable roofs, rather than the gambrel roofs required by Joseph Meacham on the early eastern meeting houses. Gable roofs were typical of early Anglo-Saxon and Scotch-Irish settlements in Ohio and Kentucky. While correspondence between eastern and western Shakers indicates a desire on the part of the western Shakers to follow eastern architectural forms, regional precedents and building knowledge prevailed.

One of the largest western meeting houses is

that of the Pleasant Hill Shakers, built in 1820 (figure 2-7). Micajah Burnett, who designed many of the buildings in this community, planned this structure in deliberate contrast to the early meeting houses in the East. A timber-frame building, the meeting house was larger than any other Shaker meeting house built at the time in the East or West until the erection of Mount Lebanon's second meeting house. Sixty feet long by forty-four feet wide, the building stands 2½ stories tall and is capped by a gable roof. Mount Lebanon's decision the following year to build their new meeting house may have been a direct response to Burnett's structure at Pleasant Hill.

All Shaker meeting houses were built of wood, except for the one constructed at Whitewater, Ohio (figure 2-8). This meeting house presents an unusual case both in its materials and its location. The village was a small settlement founded about 1824, much later than the other western communities. The closing of the West Union, Indiana, village in 1827 led to an influx of new members at Whitewater. Although it is unclear why the Shakers built their meeting house at this time, it could have been to accommodate additional Believers. The Whitewater Shakers' choice of brick for their meeting house might have violated Shaker rules concerning building materials, but there is no evidence suggesting that the Mount Lebanon ministry disapproved. When Isaac N. Youngs made his visit to the community in 1834, he noted that most of the buildings were still "poor log houses" except the meeting house and the new Center Family dwelling house, also built of brick.[10] However, he makes no judgment on the meeting house. Perhaps the Whitewater Shak-

ers chose brick because it was locally produced; they made the brick for both the meeting house and the new dwelling house at a nearby site. Aside from its materials, the Whitewater meeting house followed the design of the one at Pleasant Hill, though at 45 by 35 feet it was considerably smaller.

In 1855, with the purchase of a farm to the south of the Whitewater community, the meeting house no longer stood in the center of the village. The new farm became known as the South Family, the South Family became known as the Center Family and the Center Family, where the meeting house is located, became the North Family. Despite the change in names, the members remained at their original families and retained their original status. Though plans were made to move the structure eventually so that it would again stand in the physical center of the village, the decline of

2-8 Whitewater, Ohio, had the only brick meeting house (1827). This building resembles western dwelling houses rather than the meeting houses of the eastern Shaker communities.

2-9   The Watervliet, New York, meeting house (1847) was one of the last Shaker meeting houses built. The south facade has two entrance doors, while the north facade has three separate doors for brothers, ministry, and sisters. This arrangement followed that of the 1824 meeting house at Mount Lebanon, New York (figure 2-5).

Whitewater and its closing in 1916 prevented any action. When visiting what is left of the village today, one must travel to the northern reaches of the site to see the meeting house and the remaining buildings of the North Family.

The Last Shaker Meeting Houses

The Shakers erected their last meeting houses in 1847 at the first Shaker settlement, Watervliet, New York, and in 1848 at North Union, Ohio. Although Watervliet already had a meeting house, built in 1791, the Shakers decided to construct a larger one just south of it to accommodate the village's growing population. The wood-frame building resembles the meeting houses of the western villages in its rectilinear plan and gable roof. However, it is proportionally longer and narrower than the others, measuring 113 by 54 feet (figure 2-9). Yet it also looks to the 1824 meeting house at Mount Lebanon in the placement of three doors at the short, north end of the building to permit

2-10 The Groveland, New York, Shakers made walnut benches specifically for Watervliet's new meeting house.

separate entrances for the brothers (left), ministry (center), and sisters (right). Another innovation is the placement of raised benches along one of the short ends of the meeting room rather than along one of the long ends, as in most other meeting houses (figure 2-10). These walnut benches were made at the Groveland, New York, community and sent as a gift to Watervliet. North Union's new meeting house also followed this rectangular plan, with a foundation measuring 100 by 50 feet. Like other Believers, the North Union Shakers considered their new house of worship the symbol of community. However, they went further than other Shaker villages by having both brothers and sisters participate in the building's construction to avoid employing hired help.

Despite the variation in style owing to changes in taste, population growth, and regional differences, the meeting houses all served several important purposes. They marked the spiritual and the physical center of the community, providing not only a communal space for worship, but also representing the temporal and religious foundations upon which the Shaker faith depended. To some contemporary visitors who came to observe Sunday services, they merely provided an arena for the dances and hymns the sect performed. To others, however, the buildings symbolized the hope for salvation through architectural perfection. The neat, white meeting houses embodied the Shakers' aspirations to create a kingdom of heaven on earth.

2-11 Built by Moses Johnson, the Canterbury, New Hampshire, meeting house (1792) demonstrates the simplicity and symmetry of early Shaker buildings, which drew on both Anglo-Dutch and Federal-style architecture.

3 Dwelling Houses

Structures for Communal Life

THE MEETING HOUSES, in their function as the homes of the ministry, provided the perfect models for Shaker dwelling houses. Although house forms changed over time, the designs of the eighteenth-century Shaker dwellings were closely related to the early meeting houses. As the central structures in the daily lives of the Shakers—where they slept, ate, worked, and worshipped—these buildings needed to nurture and enforce codes of behavior. As these codes changed, so did the forms of dwellings. In this sense, dwellings most clearly reveal, in a concrete way, the shifts in religious and social practices within Shakerism.

3-1 The ubiquitous Shaker pegboard allowed clothing and furniture to be hung out of the way. Shaker cloaks, which became popular in the late nineteenth century among women of the world, hang in a cloak room in the Pleasant Hill, Kentucky, Center Family dwelling.

Early Dwelling Houses

The first buildings to shelter the Shakers were houses owned by converts to the religion. During her missionary trip to Harvard, Massachusetts, Ann Lee lived in the Shadrach Ireland House, also called the Square House (figure 3-2). According to Shaker accounts, the very first Shaker-built dwelling houses were small, poorly built structures. In the eastern communities, the Shakers adopted local Anglo-Dutch architectural forms for their dwellings, as they had with their meeting houses. Written descriptions and Shaker village views indicate these early dwellings had gambrel roofs and single entrances. Many of them had to be constructed quickly to accommodate the large influx of converts. For example, by 1790 Mount Lebanon had 221 inhabitants and only three Shaker-built dwellings in addition to an older farm house and

3-2 The Shadrach Ireland House (also called the Square House; 1769) sheltered Ann Lee and her followers during their missionary trips to Harvard, Massachusetts, in 1782 and 1783. It is the only extant building in which Mother Ann is known to have lived.

3-3 One of the larger dwellings built at Mount Lebanon, New York, the North Family dwelling house (1816; additions 1845, 1863) revealed successive phases of Shaker architecture. The Shakers favored the shallow gable roof in the mid-nineteenth century as a way to provide more space on the top floor. The Darrow School demolished this building in 1973. (Historic American Buildings Survey, Collection of the Library of Congress, Prints and Photographs Division.)

other small buildings to house its members, so that early dwellings measuring approximately 50 by 40 feet had to house perhaps twenty to forty people. At this time there was little, if any, separation of the sexes. Most Shakers, men, women, and children, lived together under crowded conditions.

As the communities became more established, the ministry at Mount Lebanon realized that larger, better organized dwellings would have to be built. In the 1820s and 1830s the Shakers undertook large building programs to erect new dwelling houses and enlarge old ones. These new dwellings were designed to help enforce rules then being established governing social behavior within the society, particularly the interaction of men and women.

The Millennial Laws

Although the Millennial Laws were not written down until 1821 and not widely circulated until 1845, many of the rules they list were in force well before 1821. The revised versions of 1845 and 1860 are better known and had a wider circulation. In addition to the prescribed hymns and dances of worship and standardized ways of speaking and dressing, rules existed that outlined conduct within dwellings. Joseph Meacham had believed that brothers and sisters should interact to remind them of the worldly vices they had given up to become celibate Shakers. His successors continued this practice. Hence, men and women lived together in dwelling houses. Consequently, Shaker elders were extremely concerned with establishing rules that would help members remain celibate while carrying out Meacham's commands. They attempted to create separate spheres within one building. A section of the Millennial Laws entitled "Orders concerning rising in the Morning and retiring to Rest at Night" contains the following rules:

> 2. Brethren should leave their rooms, within fifteen minutes after the signal time of rising in the morning, unless prevented by sickness or infirmity.

> 3. Sisters must not go to brethren's rooms, to do chores, until twenty minutes after the signal time of rising in the morning.[11]

Under "Orders concerning Intercourse between the Sexes":

> 7. Brethren and sisters may not pass each other on the stairs.

> 12. There must not be any sitting or standing on the outside steps, railings or platforms, nor in the doors, or halls to hold lengthy conversations, either of brethren with brethren, sisters with sisters, or of brethren and sisters together.[12]

These rules recognized the possibility of brothers and sisters meeting in the dwellings, but depended upon the honesty of the members and surveillance by the elders, eldresses, deacons, and deaconesses. Although the Laws circulated through most Shaker communities, they represented ideals of conduct rather than actual practices. The Millennial Laws were often difficult to enforce and their real influence in controlling behavior is difficult to measure. In 1860 the Mount Lebanon ministry changed the Laws to reflect more relaxed attitudes toward interaction between men and women and conduct in the outside world.

3-4 Staircases, South Family dwelling house (ca. 1831), Mount Lebanon, New York. The two staircases demonstrate the separate, but ostensibly equal, nature of gender roles in Shaker society. Men and women lived in the same dwellings but had separate spaces delineated by separate entrances, stairs, sitting rooms, and retiring rooms.

3-5 Kitchen, Church Family dwelling house (1830), Hancock, Massachusetts. Sisters, working in the basement kitchen of the dwelling house, produced meals for approximately one hundred inhabitants. The industrial-size kettles and ovens were already in use in institutional kitchens when the Shakers built this dwelling.

3-6 The Church Family dwelling house (1830) at Hancock was the first entirely brick dwelling to be constructed at an eastern village. Like other Shaker structures of this period, the building drew inspiration from the Federal style. Its size, windows, belfry, and plan, however, mark it as a Shaker structure.

3-7 Ammi B. Youngs, a non-Shaker and the architect of the Vermont State Capitol, designed Enfield, New Hampshire's stone dwelling house (1837–41), built of local granite.

Nineteenth-Century Eastern Dwelling Houses

Rapid construction in the 1820s, 1830s, and 1840s demonstrated the elders' desire to erect dwellings that could hold up to one hundred members and still ensure celibacy. In 1845 the North Family at Mount Lebanon doubled the size of its main dwelling house by enlarging it from 60 by 45 feet to 120 by 45 feet. The family added two stories to the house in 1863 (figure 3-3). In the 1830s the Church Family enlarged its "Great House" and the South Family erected a large, new dwelling. The increased size permitted the inclusion of separate doors and stairways for men and women (figure 3-4) as well as larger kitchen and dining facilities to house the higher number of inhabitants (figure 3-5).

Although the Millennial Laws never specified a style to be used for Shaker architecture, the society favored the Federal style and continued using it even when the outside world had moved on to other architectural styles. The Federal style was a streamlined version of Neoclassical architecture, favoring symmetrical facades and floor plans and little ornament around windows and doorways. More embellished revival styles such as the Gothic or the Egyptian clearly did not suit the Shakers' ideals of perfection and industry: the Shakers would have considered the elaborate details demanded by these styles to be superfluous. The Federal style provided an alternative in its simplicity and its relative ease of construction to the prolific ornament of revival styles. In terms of fashion, Shaker taste remained in the early nineteenth century. Architecture, furniture, and clothing reflected the popular styles of this period, changing only slightly until after the Civil War.

According to the Millennial Laws, the color of dwellings was as important as the color of meeting houses. Wood-frame dwellings were to be painted like shops, "as near uniform in color, as consistent; but it is advisable to have shops of a little darker shade than dwelling houses." Nineteenth-century drawings of Mount Lebanon and Sabbathday Lake, Maine, depict many dwellings and shops in a light yellow color. However, other drawings such as the 1833 plan of Harvard, Massachusetts, and the 1845 plan of Alfred, Maine, show that some Shaker villages painted their frame dwellings white like the meeting house (pages 16–17 and figure 1-3). Apparently, the Millennial Laws were ignored in this respect as early as the 1830s and 1840s.

Other villages erected new dwellings at this time, but departed from the original timber-frame form. The Church Family at Hancock constructed their brick dwelling, the first in the eastern communities, in 1830 (figure 3-6). Attributed to Elder William Deming, who was involved in the construction of many other buildings at the village, the four-story gable-roofed structure reflects the Federal style. The Church Family at Enfield, New Hampshire, went to even greater expense by building a dwelling out of stone (figure 3-7). In form, the structure, built between 1837 and 1841, appears much like the Hancock dwelling: four stories tall with a gable roof. Other families at the villages followed the Church Families' leads in constructing their dwellings.

Unsure as to how to construct such a large stone building, the Enfield Shaker elders and trustees consulted with many builders in places as far away

3-8 The stone dwelling house at Enfield had separate staircases for the segregated sexes, located at opposite ends of the building.

as Boston. They finally hired an outside architect, the well-known Ammi B. Youngs, who had designed the Vermont State Capitol. While such a step was unusual, Youngs designed the dwelling in the Greek Revival style, which satisfied Shaker aesthetic standards. Upon seeing the building on a visit to Enfield in 1843, Elder Giles B. Avery of Mount Lebanon could not contain his admiration: "A beautiful situation truly, but O: what a stone palace. . . . one of the most stately, magnificent, and solid buildings I ever saw."[13] By the 1840s, the Mount Lebanon ministry had loosened its

3-9 Dining room, Church Family dwelling house, Hancock, Massachusetts. Efficiency pervaded all aspects of Shaker life. The sisters used large dumbwaiters to raise and lower food, plates, and utensils between the dining room and the basement kitchen, limiting their trips up and down the stairs.

requirements that dwellings be constructed of wood.

Still standing today, the Hancock and Enfield dwellings exhibit the evolving roles of such structures in the early nineteenth century. In addition to merely providing shelter, the newer dwellings helped maintain order between brothers and sisters (figure 3-8). Although men and women lived together in the dwelling house, they had separate entrances, stairways, and sitting rooms. Their bedrooms, called "retiring rooms," were located on the same floors, but were either clustered at opposite ends of the floor or across the hall from one another. Although no walls physically divided men and

women, the dichotomy of male and female space emphasized the separate but largely equal nature of men and women in Shaker religion and society.

Dwelling houses also encompassed aspects of work and worship. Inhabitants took their meals in the communal dining room located either in the basement or on the first floor (figure 3-9). The large kitchen and storage rooms adjacent were the work sites for sisters who cooked, canned, made cheese, or prepared meals (figures 3-10, 3-11, 3-12). The upper floors sometimes housed small shops for spinning, weaving, or sewing, though these tasks were often performed in a separate workshop, the sisters' shop.

The most important communal space in the dwelling was the meeting room. Usually this room was located on the second or third floor above the dining room. Like the worship space in the meeting house, the meeting room had no freestanding columns or other structural supports to obstruct the movements of Shaker dances (figure 3-23, pages 64–65). Some eastern dwellings, such as the one at Hancock or the South Family dwelling house at Watervliet, New York, had panels stored inside the upper walls which could be lowered to divide the meeting room into smaller spaces (figure 3-13). This room not only functioned as the site of daily family worship, but it also provided space for smaller meetings. As the religious fervor of Shakerism diminished after the 1840s, the meeting

3-10 Basement preserve room, Church Family dwelling house, Hancock. Sisters preserved fruit and vegetables in the basement of the dwelling house. The stone walls and floor kept the room cool.

3-11 Kitchen, Center Family dwelling house, Pleasant Hill, Kentucky. Shelves and pegboards kept jugs and bottles in order and made cooking and serving food more efficient for the sisters. Unlike Hancock's Church Family dwelling, where the kitchen is located below the dining room, the Center Family dwelling's kitchen stands adjacent to the dining room, seen here through the arched doorway.

rooms were used less for worship and more for lectures on topics such as spiritualism and pacifism, singing practice, and even theatrical events, such as Christmas pageants. A small stage can still be seen in the meeting room of Canterbury's main dwelling house (figure 3-15).

The most important function of the dwelling house was to shape behavior to conform to Shaker laws. Like the viewing windows in the meeting houses, which allowed elders to observe the worship activities of the community, the floor plans of the dwellings permitted surveillance of members by family elders. Two elders and two eldresses lived in each dwelling; the two men shared a retiring room, as did the two women. Usually their quarters were located on the first floor near the front or rear entrances. In the morning and in the evening, when the brothers and sisters were waking up or preparing to go to sleep, the elders could insure that everyone occupied his or her appropriate place and did not linger in the halls or talk needlessly. Deacons and deaconesses, male and female officers who attended to the temporal needs of each family, also resided in prominent rooms in the dwelling. Since four to eight brothers or sisters shared a retiring room, the lack of privacy made conversations and secret meetings difficult, though not impossible.

There is considerable variation in the layout of entrance doors to dwelling houses. While most large dwellings have separate entrances for brothers and sisters following the order in meeting houses—left for brothers, right for sisters—some dwellings at each village had single entrances. Even significant dwellings such as the Church Family's main house at Watervliet, or the Center House at Union Village, had only a single front entrance (figure 3-16). The use of this type of door placement may have come from local construction prac-

3-12 Kitchen, Church Family dwelling house, Hancock. Located in the basement of the dwelling house, the kitchen provided a comfortable place for sisters to work. Large windows lit and cooled the room.

3-13 Double doors, one for sisters, one for brothers, led into the meeting room from the hall of the Church Family dwelling house at Hancock. Wood panels stored in the walls above could be lowered into the room to divide it into three smaller rooms.

3-14 The dining room in Pleasant Hill's Center Family dwelling house contains stylistic elements borrowed from worldly architecture, such as the fanlight over the kitchen door and the Tuscan columns.

tices with which Shaker builders were familiar. The Mount Lebanon ministry encouraged Believers elsewhere to follow models established at that village, but as we have already seen, families at other communities often chose to deviate from Shaker standards to meet their own needs.

By the 1840s the dwelling houses dominated Shaker villages through their size, height, location, and the cupolas atop their roofs (figure 3-17). Those of the principal Shaker families of each village, the Church or Center Families, stood directly across the street from the meeting houses or near them (figure 3-18). Families erected additional dwellings as required. Each family paid for its own buildings unless it needed help from a more prosperous family such as the Church Family. Often family elders and brethren, experienced in building, supervised and performed the work. However, for large projects, brothers from other families might offer assistance if they could spare the labor, or the family hired outside workers.

Nineteenth-Century Western Dwelling Houses

A comparison of dwelling houses in the East and West provides the most striking contrast in regional styles and construction practices among Shaker building types. When most western communities were settled in the first decade of the nineteenth century, Kentucky, Ohio, and Indiana were still very much at the American frontier. The earliest Shaker dwellings there consisted of rough log cabins. As in the eastern villages, rapid growth required the construction of more permanent buildings. Soon even these became too small. The

3-15 Meeting room, Church Family dwelling house (1793; additions until 1837), Canterbury, New Hampshire. Over the years the Canterbury Shakers altered their meeting room to accommodate lectures and theatrical performances. A platform at the front of the room served as a stage, while ceiling lamps illuminated evening events. (Historic American Buildings Survey, Collection of the Library of Congress, Prints and Photographs Division.)

3-16 The Center Family dwelling house (1844) at Union Village, Ohio, is constructed of Shaker-made brick. It is one of only two Shaker buildings remaining at the former Center Family site, now a retirement home. The Shakers added the front porch and the roof over the side door in the late nineteenth century to make the building more fashionable.

3-18 The Pleasant Hill, Kentucky, Shakers built their Center Family dwelling house (left) across the road from the meeting house, a typical arrangement in Shaker villages.

3-19 Originally built as a dwelling house, the limestone Farm Deacons' shop (1809) was the first permanent structure erected by the Shakers at Pleasant Hill, Kentucky. After the Shakers constructed newer dwellings, they used the building as a tavern and later as the Farm Deacons' shop.

first permanent dwelling erected at Pleasant Hill in 1809, was a small, central-stair, 2½-story, gable-roofed structure made of limestone, an abundant material in the Kentucky River valley (figure 3-19). The Pleasant Hill Shakers used limestone primarily for the buildings of the Center Family, the most prominent family in the village. The whiteness of the stone and its durability enhanced the sense of permanence and prosperity that the Shakers sought to project. The Center Family soon outgrew its first dwelling house. The farm deacons later used the building and it is known today as the Farm Deacons' House.

The western dwelling houses constructed in the 1820s and 1830s tended to be more elaborate than those in the East for a number of reasons. First, many of them are larger because of kitchen ells that extend from the back of the dwellings. These ells evolved from detached kitchens, known as summer kitchens, set behind the main house. In addition to being a popular means of confining fire danger and pests in the warm months, the detached kitchen was a traditional form among continental European settlers in the Midwest. Detached kitchens

3-17 Built in 1793 as a small, gambrel-roofed house, Canterbury's Church Family dwelling evolved into a large, 3½-story dwelling by the late 1830s. The octagonal cupola was one of the more elaborate features seen on a Shaker dwelling. The Mount Lebanon ministry considered the cupola too worldly, so the Canterbury Shakers cut the belfry's height by 5 feet, 5 inches to give it a more restrained appearance.

3-20 High ceilings and wide hallways in the Center Family dwelling house at Pleasant Hill, Kentucky, kept the interior cool and fostered a light, airy feeling.

were not common in the Northeast. Though they gave no reason, the Mount Lebanon ministry most likely insisted that kitchens be connected to the dwellings so that the buildings in the West would conform more closely to those in the East. Nevertheless, Isaac N. Youngs's maps show that some families at the villages of North Union, Watervliet (Ohio), Whitewater, and South Union continued to maintain separate kitchens in log cabins located behind dwelling houses as late as the 1830s. However, the larger and wealthier families of the western communities followed Mount Lebanon's requirement which, in the West, resulted in the addition of rear kitchen ells on most dwellings. These ells also housed the dining room, the meeting room, and additional retiring rooms.

In addition to influencing the construction of separate kitchens, the warmer climate of the South also shaped Shaker architecture: large windows, high ceilings, and wide hallways encouraged air circulation in the houses of western communities (figure 3-20). These features are seen in Shaker buildings as well as worldly structures.

The grand appearance of some western dwellings stems from the western Shakers' preference for building in brick or stone rather than in wood. These materials were more abundant locally and less costly than timber. Mount Lebanon initially tried to prevent the use of brick and stone in the West since it was not in "church order," that is, such materials did not conform to the eastern ministry's rules concerning architecture. Correspondence between South Union and Mount Lebanon reveals the friction over this issue. During the construction of the Center Family's dwelling house from 1822 to 1833, the Kentucky Shakers

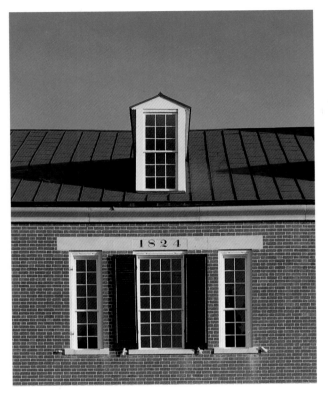

3-21 The Center Family brick dwelling house (1822–33) at South Union, Kentucky, presented a prosperous appearance to visitors with its dormers and stone lintels.

3-22 Large timbers support the roof of South Union's Center Family dwelling house. Despite a nineteenth-century fire in the attic, the building remains structurally sound.

argued that wood was scarce and brick plentiful:

> But generally speaking perhaps where there is
> any particular disadvantage in any country . . .
> in any necessary thing for the comfort and
> support of life, there is also found some substi-
> tute or remedy for this disadvantage. This is
> much the case with us in regard to building
> materials—we are much put to it for a little
> building timber, as it is extremely scarce here . . .
> but good building stone of different kinds & the
> best kind of materials for brick, we have conven-
> ient & in plenty.[14]

Despite Mount Lebanon's protests, the South
Union Shakers prevailed. They used brick for the
supporting walls and framed the roof in wood (figures 3-21 and 3-22). As has been noted earlier,
eastern communities such as Hancock and Enfield,
New Hampshire, soon built their own dwellings of
brick or stone.

Micajah Burnett, a trustee of Pleasant Hill who
supervised many of the community's construction
projects, is largely responsible for the worldly elegance of many of the western dwellings. A remark-
able man and talented builder, Burnett combined
the Shaker requirements of dual spaces for men
and women with the architectural forms and
details of the Federal style as they appeared in
nearby public and institutional buildings. His use
of fanlights over the front entrance of the North

3-23 An arched ceiling gracefully spans the open space of the
meeting room in the Center Family dwelling at Pleasant Hill,
Kentucky. Large windows and an arched transom above the
room's entrance bring light and air into the meeting space.

3-24 Built-in cupboards and drawers provided storage space for members as well as limiting what each could possess. These built-ins are in the sisters' waiting room in the Church Family dwelling at Hancock. Waiting rooms functioned as places to assemble before meals or other events in the dwelling house.

Lot Family's second dwelling (ca. 1816) and in the meeting room and dining room of the Center Family's third dwelling house (1824-34) reveal his skill in manipulating light (figure 3-23). Mary Rae Chemotti has argued that these fanlights, and the incorporation of freestanding and attached Tuscan columns in the dining room, indicate Burnett's knowledge of architectural details in buildings such as the Old State Capitol in Frankfort, Kentucky (figure 3-14).[13] Burnett made numerous trips to the city in his capacity as trustee and thus had many opportunities to study the architecture there.

3-25 Large counters with drawers provided additional storage in the attic of the Center Family dwelling at Pleasant Hill, Kentucky. The stair to the right leads to a dormer which opens to the roof.

Shaker Furniture

Now admired for its design, the original purpose of Shaker furniture, both built-in and movable, has been forgotten. These pieces provided another means of control within the dwelling. Rooms had a limited number of drawers and cupboards (figure 3-24). These objects were built into the walls, determining the amount of personal storage space each Shaker had, thereby limiting accumulation of possessions. This arrangement also required roommates to share storage space with

3-26 Retiring room, Center Family dwelling house, Pleasant Hill. Brothers and sisters slept in the same dwelling house, but in separate retiring rooms. Initially, Shakers of the same sex slept together in double beds, but at the urging of family elders, brothers made enough single beds to accommodate members in most villages by the mid-nineteenth century.

each other. Such cooperation promoted selflessness. Common storage spaces, located in attics, also prevented members from concealing personal effects (figure 3-25). The ubiquitous.pegboard also provided storage for clothing, but offered no privacy (figure 3-1, page 48). In addition, rules regarding movable furniture controlled space and made it difficult for a Shaker to arrange a room to

suit his or her tastes. Under "Orders concerning Furniture in Retiring Rooms" the Millennial Laws outlined what items could be used in these rooms and how they should look:

2. Bedsteads should be painted green,— Comfortables [comforters] should be of a modest color, not checked, striped or flowered.

Blankets or Comfortables for out side spreads, should be blue and white, but not checked or striped; other kinds now in use may be worn out.

3. One rocking chair in a room is sufficient, except where the aged reside. One table, one or two stands, a lamp stand may be attached to the woodwork, if desired. One good looking glass, which ought not to exceed eighteen inches in length, and twelve in width, with a plain frame.

7. No maps, Charts, and no pictures or paint ings, shall ever be hung up in your dwelling-rooms, shops, or Office. And no pictures or paintings set in frames, with glass before them shall ever be among you.[16] (Figures 3-26 and 3-27.)

Like the Millennial Laws concerning buildings, these rules do not specify the type of furniture permitted. It is likely that interiors were not furnished completely with Shaker-made pieces, but mixed with chairs and other objects from the outside world. Many converts brought belongings, including pieces of furniture, with them when they entered the sect. According to Shaker records, possessions of new members were inventoried and either used or discarded.

3-27 Retiring room, Church Family dwelling house, Hancock. Only small mirrors were permitted in retiring rooms in the early nineteenth century. Over the years, Shaker rules became difficult to enforce and the ministry allowed larger mirrors, even paintings and books, in retiring rooms.

3-28 Called the Great House (1875–77), this large brick dwelling replaced the first Church Family house destroyed in a fire in 1875 at Mount Lebanon, New York. One of the last and grandest Shaker dwellings to be built, the Great House had modern conveniences such as gas lighting and central heating.

3-29 Meeting room, Church Family dwelling house, Mount Lebanon. Like the meeting room at Pleasant Hill, Kentucky, this worship space has an arched ceiling and numerous windows to let in light. Bent-plywood benches purchased from Gardner and Company of New York fill the room. Shaker chairs can be seen against the walls. William Winter took this photograph in the 1920s, when Shakers still lived at the village. (Historic American Buildings Survey, Collection of the Library of Congress, Prints and Photographs Division.)

Communal Living Arrangements in Dwelling Houses

As families grew, sometimes to a few hundred members, they built dwellings to house specific age groups, particularly children and the elderly. Normally, children lived in separate buildings called Children's Houses. Often they were segregated even further into Boys' and Girls' Houses. Here guardians of the same sex watched over young Shakers until they were old enough to live with adult members, at age sixteen for boys and fourteen for girls. Sometimes boys and girls lived in retiring rooms in the upper floors of brethren's or sisters' workshops. When children moved into the main dwellings, they were placed in retiring rooms with brothers and sisters who would serve as models of behavior and continue to train the

youths in various tasks. This practice separated children who were learning to become Shakers from adult Shakers. Children who entered communities with their parents were usually separated from their blood relatives to form new relationships with their spiritual brothers and sisters. Often this separation lasted until children became covenanted Shakers or left the sect.

Likewise, the elderly and infirm lived apart from the main body of Shakers. There was no specific age at which an aged member left the main dwelling. Instead, the physical and mental health of a member determined where he or she lived. When a Shaker reached a point at which physical labor was impossible, he or she moved to the home for the aged. This practice followed the custom of housing members according to their labor roles. Men who worked in the fields often shared rooms. Women who worked in the laundry also lived together. Elderly sisters who did mending and other light tasks might share rooms in the main house or live together in the house for the aged.

The governing role one played within Shaker society also determined where one lived. Most Shakers lived in one of the main dwellings of their family. The ministry elders and eldresses lived in the meeting house. Trustees, Shaker brothers who dealt regularly with the world in handling the society's business affairs, also lived apart from the rest

3-30 Meeting room, Sabbathday Lake dwelling house. Meeting rooms in dwelling houses provided a place for Shaker families to worship during the week. By the late nineteenth century, chairs from the outside world supplemented Shaker benches. Another worldly feature is the stenciled cornice pattern.

The Victorianization of Dwelling Houses

The dwelling houses constructed after the Civil War were elaborate affairs in comparison to the earlier dwellings. Because of the decline in the number of Shakers, particularly men, many building projects relied more than ever on hired help. In addition, the Shakers' changing aesthetic desires, strongly influenced by Victorian style (that catch-all term for the Queen Anne and Eastlake styles of the second half of the nineteenth century), and a growing dependence on goods from the outside world encouraged a higher degree of decoration.

3-31 Kitchen, Sabbathday Lake dwelling house. Shakers continue to embrace modern technology while preserving elements of their past.

At Mount Lebanon, the Church Family's new Great House, built to replace the first one (burned in a disastrous fire in 1875), exemplifies this change in style (figure 3-28). Designed by Elders Giles B. Avery and George Wickersham, the large, T-shaped, brick Great House is reminiscent of the brick and stone dwellings of Kentucky in both material and form. The elders may have hoped to recapture the appearance of the prosperous 1830s and 1840s by looking back to building forms favored in that period. They furnished the house with many conveniences and objects from the outside world, creating an interior that resembled the homes of affluent nonbelievers rather than the heretofore austere Shakers. A forced-air heating system and hot and cold running water provided amenities most Americans did not yet have in their homes. With its marble-topped dining tables and bent-plywood meeting room benches, the Great House provided more luxurious quarters than the Shakers had ever experienced (figure 3-29). Perhaps the most significant departure from many

of the Shakers. They resided in the village's office, the building where outsiders stopped if they wanted to see the trustees, visit the community, or buy Shaker goods. In the 1830s and 1840s many Shaker families experienced events called "great moves," when members were moved from room to room or from house to house. Death, apostasy, age, or elevation of a brother or sister to the position of elder or eldress for a family or for the ministry spurred these reorganizations. When children reached an age of maturity, they moved into houses with adults to continue their Shaker education. The aged moved at these times as well. Often Shakers changed their tasks at this time, too, moving into retiring rooms with new companions with whom they would work.

3-32 By the late nineteenth century, Shakers had acquired the tastes of the outside world. Walnut chairs, tables, and armoires purchased from furniture companies filled Shaker rooms, as seen in the Center Family dwelling house at South Union, Kentucky.

earlier Shaker dwellings at Mount Lebanon was the lack of double doors for men and women. While other families and other communities had used single entrance doors in their buildings, the decision not to use double doors for the main dwelling at the Church Family, the first family at Mount Lebanon, marked a significant step away from earlier, more restrictive forms of building. The new Great House had only one front entrance door, spanned by a large fanlight—further evidence of the relaxation of Shaker values. This house prompted the construction of similar houses at Enfield, Connecticut (1876) and at Sabbathday Lake (1883–84). (Page 11) The Shakers at

Sabbathday Lake seem to have specifically wanted a more up-to-date dwelling. In 1882 they demolished their wood-frame dwelling, originally built in 1795 and subsequently enlarged, to make room for their new brick house (figure 3-30).

The last dwelling house built for the Shakers was the "Big House" in White Oak, Georgia. Constructed in 1899, the building bore little resemblance to earlier Shaker dwellings. Instead, it looked like a large Stick-style mansion with its gabled projecting bays and vertical decorative trim. Built of pine, oak, and walnut, the house, measuring nearly 90 by 40 feet, was designed to accommodate fifty or more members. However, as Dale Covington has noted, the Shakers' optimism in planning for a thriving new village was ill-founded; in 1900 only eleven people resided in the community.[17]

The Shakers continued to change with the times. Unlike some communal sects, they embraced new technology. The Shakers added gas lighting, central heating, electricity, telephones, and other modern conveniences to their dwellings as soon as they could (figure 3-31). Although these additions made daily life easier, they increased the difficulty of maintaining self-sufficiency and spiritual isolation. By choosing to use the latest technology, the Shakers became more strongly linked to the outside world, depending on companies to provide new products and to service old ones.

Shaker Dwelling Houses in the Twentieth Century

Nevertheless, the continued use of the dwelling houses in the twentieth century attests to their adaptability. Photographs in the Historic American Buildings Survey show how the Shakers inhabited these buildings in the 1920s and 1930s. By this time, only a few elderly brothers and sisters lived in dwellings that had been built to accommodate one hundred or more Shakers. Instead of interiors sparsely furnished with Shaker pieces, early twentieth-century photographs of sisters' retiring rooms at Mount Lebanon and Watervliet show a mixture of Shaker and worldly furnishings. Although the Millennial Laws had prohibited pictures, books, and carpets, Shaker lives had changed so much that interiors resembled those of the mainstream middle class (figure 3-32).

For much of the twentieth century, the main dwellings at the last two living Shaker communities, Canterbury and Sabbathday Lake, have been home to Shakers. Until her death in 1992, Sister Ethel Hudson lived alone in the large Church Family dwelling at Canterbury. She chose to inhabit the two front rooms on the first floor of the house, leaving the rest of the building empty. Closed off from visitors during Sister Ethel's lifetime, the building will eventually become part of the Shaker museum at Canterbury. The house provides the perfect opportunity to offer a public example of a Shaker dwelling as it changed over nearly two hundred years of use. The brick house at Sabbathday Lake is the last Shaker dwelling to shelter Believers. Some of the members live in it and the entire community takes its meals in the communal dining room (figure 3-33). At this village and at the other Shaker communities that are now museums, the dwelling houses continue to dominate the landscape, a testimony to the Shakers' communal experiment.

3-33 The Shaker brothers and sisters living at Sabbathday Lake today continue to dine at separate tables in the dining room of the 1883 dwelling house.

4 Offices and Stores

Interaction with the World

THE SHAKER OFFICE, also known as the trustees' office because it housed Shaker officers of that name, served a unique purpose in the community. The building, and the trustees who inhabited it, embodied the link between the Shakers and the world. Though visitors were free to pass through the village — indeed, this was necessary as main highways intersected most Shaker villages — visitors stopped at the office to request to tour the village or spend the night. Sometimes a store selling Shaker products like herbs, textiles, or fancy goods such as pin cushions or sewing kits, was housed in or attached to the office (figure 4-1). Other times the store was a separate building that stood near the office to attract the attention of visitors. At some villages there was a separate structure called the visitors' house that accommodated guests. Some families had their own office, and every village had at least one office. The situation varied from village to village depending upon the size and prosperity of the community and its relations with the outside world.

Early Offices and Stores

Unlike meeting houses and dwelling houses, offices were not erected in the earliest years of Shaker communities. Only after the village and the temporal roles of the members themselves had been defined could such buildings be conceived and built. The Shakers erected their first offices in the Church or Center Families of the villages along the main roads near the main dwelling houses. Because these settings located the offices in or near the

4-1 Store, trustees' office (1813; remodeled 1895), Hancock, Massachusetts. The Shakers sold goods such as cloaks, seeds, herbs, and postcards in their stores, which were usually housed in the village office.

hearts of the villages, the offices drew outsiders into the communities instead of keeping them on the peripheries. The Shakers displayed the prosperity of their villages in a way that gave visitors a good look, but controlled their access to specific structures.

According to written accounts and Shaker drawings, the first offices were small 1 to 2½-story frame buildings. Most often they had only one front entrance door since only brothers, the trustees, lived in them. The Shakers prohibited women from serving as trustees because they did not want them to deal directly with the world. However, the decline of the male Shaker population over the nineteenth century eventually required women to serve as trustees by the 1890s. As Shaker society became more complex, the offices became large structures within the communities. Their increased size reflected the greater importance of the Shakers' economic interests as well as the sect's interaction with the world.

The offices at eastern communities were long rectangular buildings with separate entrances at either end of the facade. Though many offices were wood-frame buildings, others were a combination of brick and wood or, in some cases, just brick. In 1827 the Church Family at Mount Lebanon built its 3½-story office (figure 4-2). The stone foundation supports two stories of brick and a wood-frame attic. The office, in its combination of brick and wood, resembles the South Family's main dwelling house. At Watervliet, New York, the Church Family Shakers decided to build a new brick office to replace their tiny one-story wood office. The new office, built in 1830, stood 56 by 44 feet and 2½ stories tall on a stone foundation.

It also held a prominent position near the junction of the Albany-Schenectady road and the main road leading into the Church Family.

Like other Shaker buildings, the office type reflected regional differences and the shifting nature of the Shakers' relationship with the outside world. Offices in the West had rear ells, whereas the eastern structures followed a rectangular plan. In addition, the western offices tended to be very large, nearly as large as the main dwelling houses, so they were a much stronger physical presence in western villages than were the offices in eastern villages. The most elegant offices are those still standing at Pleasant Hill, Kentucky, and Union Village, Ohio (now known as the Otterbein Homes and owned by the United Methodist Church). These structures, with their kitchen ells, are nearly as big as the largest of the great dwelling houses at their communities. Even the Shakers at the small village of Whitewater, Ohio, constructed a three-story office in 1855 that measured 45 by 30 feet, with a two-story rear ell of 43 by 22 feet.

Relations with the Outside World

Once the office was established as a place where visitors could eat and sleep, the building had to accommodate both brothers, as trustees, and sisters, as "office sisters" who took care of visitors. These Shakers could not live in the dwelling

4-2 Church Family trustees' office (1827), Mount Lebanon, New York. By building a separate structure to serve as their office and store, the Shakers acknowledged the importance of trade with the world. This building stands a short distance from the meeting house and main dwelling house.

4-3 The Canterbury, New Hampshire, trustees' office (1830–32) repeats the rectangular shape of the slightly earlier Mount Lebanon office. The separate entrances led into the office and store. Porches and a porte-cochere are late nineteenth-century additions.

houses because the elders feared their daily contact with outsiders might corrupt other Shakers. Shaker rules did not require offices to have separate entrances, though it appears that many had separate stairways for men and women. Buildings that had two front entrances had dual functions as both offices and visitors' lodgings (figure 4-3). One side of the building held the trustees' offices and their quarters. The other side held the store and the office sisters' quarters. Also present were sitting rooms, a visitors' dining room, a kitchen, and retiring rooms for visitors on the upper floors. The sitting rooms provided not only a place for business meetings but also a space for Shakers to visit with non-Shaker relatives excluded from the dwelling houses. The office served another important function as a place where individuals considering conversion to Shakerism could stay. When villages had a separate visitors' house, outsiders stayed in it and were cared for by the sisters who lived there. Although the trustees and sisters who lived in the office were supposed to remain separate from the rest of the Shakers because of their interaction with outsiders, these members often played important roles within the community. One such individual was Micajah Burnett, who shaped the appearance of Pleasant Hill in the first half of the nineteenth century.

Depending on the size of the community, a Shaker village could have just one office or an office for each family. Regardless of how many there were, each office held a central location within the village or family, right alongside the road. In some of the larger Shaker villages, the office often accommodated a post office for the Shaker village, as at Mount Lebanon and Canterbury, New Hampshire. Post offices were established in the mid to late nineteenth century to accommodate the large populations and therefore the large amounts of mail flowing in and out of these villages. In addition, the growing mail-order businesses at communities like Mount Lebanon demanded separate post offices. The public function of the office demanded that the building be easily accessible to visitors. It also had to present a good appearance, as it was usually the first building a visitor entered upon arrival. Aside from the meeting house, which was usually open to the public during Sunday worship meetings, the office was the only other Shaker building that visitors could officially enter.

The office at South Union, Kentucky, differed from those at other Shaker villages in that it stood apart from the core of the community in what the Shakers called the "Office Premises." Demolished long ago, the site is best known through Isaac N. Youngs's description and a copy of his map of South Union. This area encompassed a blacksmith's shop, a shed, the office, and a visitors' house. Some Shakers lived in the house and ran it as a public inn, often keeping boarders who stayed for months, bringing extra income to the community. The most unusual structure was a sort of gazebo, called a "piazza," that provided a relaxing place for guests to sit outdoors. Although the arrangement does not seem to fit in with that of the other Shaker villages, Mount Lebanon may have tolerated South Union's "Office Premises" because they provided good income for the village.

One of the most elegant Shaker buildings is the office or trustees' house at Pleasant Hill, Kentucky, designed and built by Micajah Burnett from 1839 to 1841 (figure 4-4). Double spiral staircases wind gracefully upward for three stories, ending at a landing topped by an oval dome lit by two dormers (figure 4-5). This type of stair exists nowhere else in Shakerdom, though similar stairs appear in non-Shaker houses in and around Lexington that Burnett may have seen in his travels as Center Family trustee.

The Victorianization of Shaker Offices

Other offices were transformed as Shaker villages adopted highly decorative forms of Victorianism. Two prime examples of Shaker Victorian are the offices at Hancock, Massachusetts, and at

4-4 Designed by Micajah Burnett, the Pleasant Hill, Kentucky, office (1839–41) features a fanlight and dormers, typical of worldly Federal architecture. Its stately appearance lent a prosperous air to the village.

Union Village, Ohio. The Shakers originally constructed both buildings in the early nineteenth century as large, symmetrical structures that conformed to the sect's use of the Federal style. However, by the end of the nineteenth century, the Shakers had transformed both buildings into Victorian structures complete with cupolas, towers, and decorative shingles. The Hancock Shakers began converting their office in 1895. In addition to the newly elaborate exterior, the interior gained rich carpets, wallpaper, horsehair furniture, and dark walnut and mahogany chests (figure 4-6). The Shakers victorianized some of the chests already in the building with additions of dark walnut trim and

4-5 Dormers allow light into the central hall of the trustees' office at Pleasant Hill, illuminating the unique double curved staircases below.

the replacement of wood knobs by porcelain or brass knobs (figure 4-7).

The Shakers' reasons for spending time and money to renovate their office may have been largely economic. The 1876 Centennial Exposition in Philadelphia helped disseminate nostalgia for America's colonial past. This movement, eventually known as the Colonial Revival, sought to recapture a rustic past in response to the industrialized nation the United States was rapidly becoming. The Shakers had been making and selling products to the world since the late eighteenth century; the

4-7   Changes to Hancock's office included alterations to Shaker furniture, such as replacing wood knobs with porcelain drawer pulls on large cases. The large mirror reflects a view of the parlor.

Colonial Revival brought new interest in many of the Shakers' objects—among them chairs, oval boxes, baskets, and cloaks—as representative of an idyllic past. This rise in popularity changed the

4-6   The Hancock Shakers built a simple rectangular structure as their office in 1813. A renovation in 1895 brought worldly influences including wallpaper, elaborate door moldings, staircases, and furniture. Beyond the entrance hall stands a teller cage and a safe.

way the Shakers marketed their goods. In the late eighteenth and early nineteenth centuries, the sect often sold goods on consignment in local stores or sent brothers on long trips from town to town who returned after all the merchandise had been sold. By the 1860s the Shakers had become much more sophisticated, selling their furniture wholesale to retailers in cities like Boston and New York. Soon after, they began publishing catalogs of their wares to be sold by mail.[18] In addition, Shaker villages themselves became increasingly popular tourist sites. Despite the public demand for simple things, the Shakers wished to modernize their own buildings by updating them with the proceeds from this commercial success.

The most astonishing transformation of an office took place at Union Village, Ohio. In the 1890s Elder Joseph Slingerland, a Shaker from Mount Lebanon who had moved west to help lead Union Village, played a major role in the rebuilding of the community after a severe cyclone destroyed many structures in 1886. As part of the reconstruction, he decided to renovate the unassuming office to display Shaker prosperity. The office had originally been built as one of the first dwelling houses at the village in 1810. After the Shakers built a new brick Center House in 1844, the family used their old dwelling as an office. The renovation project hid virtually every hint of the original building,

4-8 Trustees' office (1810; remodeled after 1886), Union Village, Ohio. After the Shakers remodeled their office in Union Village, the building became known as "Marble Hall" because of the extensive interior use of marble for flooring and sinks. Originally built as a plain wood-frame dwelling, the structure received two towers, a mansard roof, and a tall cupola, making it the most elaborate building at any Shaker village.

though the new structure retained its symmetrical facade. The office gained a mansard roof, two round towers, a tall cupola, and decorative porches over the entrances (figure 4-8). So much marble was used on the floors and sinks that the building immediately became known as "Marble Hall." The imposing structure stands in stark contrast to the brick 1844 Center House next to it.

The offices at Canterbury and Sabbathday Lake have continued to perform their original functions as offices and stores. Until Sister Ethel Hudson's death at Canterbury in 1992, that village was still considered a living community, though it was already functioning largely as a museum. The office (1830–32) is still the first stop for a visitor wishing to tour the site. Likewise, the office (1816) at Sabbathday Lake continues to serve as the place where visitors can inquire about Shakerism, or purchase Shaker goods and postcards of the village (figure 4-9).

4-9 The trustees' office at Sabbathday Lake, Maine, functions as it has since the Shakers built it: as an office and store. Visitors to Sabbathday Lake can still buy Shaker goods, such as herbs and seeds, here.

5 Barns, Stables, and Sheds

Agriculture and Innovation

SOME OF THE MOST well-known Shaker structures were, and still are, the large barns that functioned as the center of agricultural activities at Shaker villages. These structures, often much bigger than their non-Shaker counterparts, attracted a great deal of attention among outsiders. Shaker innovations in barn construction were featured in such nineteenth-century agricultural journals as *The Genesee Farmer* and *The American Agriculturalist* as examples of new and more efficient ways of farming. The Shakers subscribed to these journals and undoubtedly borrowed ideas from their articles on farming. However, Shaker barns, stables, and sheds, like other Shaker buildings, drew on the rur-

al architecture surrounding the villages. The Shakers took a standard form and basically enlarged it to accommodate the larger herds that their communal economies supported, as at Enfield, New Hampshire (figure 5-2). However, the sect also built experimental barns. One of these, the famous round barn at Hancock, is the only such structure in Shakerdom and was recognized in contemporary agricultural journals as an innovation (figure 5-3).

Early Barns

The earliest barns the Shakers used were buildings already standing on land given to the society by converts. The earliest Shaker-built barns, erected in the late eighteenth century, were crudely and quickly assembled structures, like many other early Shaker buildings. The communities, attempting to establish settlements, did what they could with

5-1 The Pleasant Hill, Kentucky, Shaker landscape included tobacco barns to dry the plant, a cash crop throughout the state. Although Shaker rules later banned the practice, many Believers continued to smoke.

5-2 The Enfield, New Hampshire, Shakers' large cow barn (1854) still stands. While the barn's timber-frame construction and rectangular form followed worldly building practices, its size demonstrates the importance and communal nature of agriculture in the Shaker economy.

limited resources. However, as the Shakers became more prosperous, their barns, like their other buildings, were better designed and better constructed.

Shaker Barns and Economies of Scale

The Shakers built most of their barns of wood, the most available material and the easiest to use. Aside from the round barn at Hancock, all Shaker barns were long rectangular structures two or more stories tall and usually built into a hillside so that they could be entered at different levels. On level ground the Shakers erected large earthen ramps that led into the various stories of the barn. These enormous buildings spoke to the communal ideal underlying the economy of the society.

Each family in a village had at least one main barn, although the largest usually stood at the Church or Center Family. As work buildings they were often, though not always, set back on secondary roads behind the main buildings of the village. The Millennial Laws further differentiated these structures from more prominent buildings like the meeting houses and the dwelling houses in "Concerning Building, Painting, Varnishing and the Manufacture of Articles for Sale, &c. &c." with the following rule:

> 7. Barns and back buildings, as wood houses, etc. if painted at all, should be of a dark hue, either red, or brown, lead color, or something of the kind, unless they front the road, or command a sightly aspect, and then they should not be of a very light color.[19]

The attention given to barns demonstrates the important function they had in Shaker communities, not only in a practical sense, but also to enhance the overall image of the Shaker village as a place of industry and prosperity.

Typical Shaker Barns

Shaker barns usually followed the rectangular shapes of worldly barns. An example of this type of barn is the Church Family cow barn at Enfield, New Hampshire (figure 5-2). Built from 1853 to 1854, the structure measures nearly 53 by 141 feet

5-3 The heavy timbers and thick stone walls of the Hancock, Massachusetts, round barn display the building's solid construction. Hatches in the floor allowed brethren to shovel manure into the cellar. In addition to acting as fertilizer, the manure produced heat to help keep the barn warm in the winter.

and stands on a foundation of randomly laid granite. Heavy wood timbers support the frame, which is three bays wide and eight bays long and follows the standard form of New England barn construction for the period. The structure retains its original polychrome slate roof with the date "1854" outlined in blue slate. The barn itself stands on a slightly sloped site that allows earthen ramps to abut the three-story structure on two different levels. Cows were kept on the first level. Wagons bearing hay could drive onto the second level via a ramp, unload the hay into the stalls below, and then exit out the other end of the barn. In this way, the barn functioned efficiently by providing easy access and using gravity to save labor. The Shakers' concern with light and air circulation (a safeguard against fire) is seen in the numerous windows piercing the walls of the barn, the vents in the roof, and the cupola rising over the central part of the building.

Experimental Barns

The Hancock Shakers built their round barn in 1826 with an internal wood frame and curved exterior stone walls (figure 5-4). A fire on December 1, 1864, destroyed the barn's original conical roof and substructure. The Shakers subsequently altered the upper level by adding a circular loft and an octagonal louvered cupola to let in light and air. They also replaced much of the internal framework

5-4 The round barn at Hancock (1826; rebuilt 1865) is the only one of its type in all of Shakerdom. The circular layout made work more efficient by enabling one brother to perform tasks, such as feeding cows, which required several men in a conventional barn.

at this time. Most unusual is the central shaft that rises up through the three levels of the barn and supports the cupola (figure 5-5). In the late nineteenth century the Shakers added a carriage shed, and in the early twentieth century a cattle shed. By the early 1960s, after the remaining Shakers had left the site, the barn fell into disrepair, but an intensive restoration effort on the part of Hancock Shaker Village has successfully returned the building to its 1865 appearance.

Hancock's round barn exemplifies the Shaker spirit of efficient production and the sect's love of order. Cattle were kept on the main floor along the perimeter surrounding a central hay mow, and hay was stored on the second floor. Earthen ramps led into the barn on each of these two levels. Thus, wagons loaded with hay could be driven into the barn on the second floor. One brother alone could toss the hay down into the hay mow below, feeding all the cows in a short time (figure 5-3). Manure could be collected on the lowest level, below the cows, and hauled out to fields to be used as fertilizer. Although the Shakers considered the round barn a success, no other round barns were constructed at Shaker villages because the shape defied the Mount Lebanon ministry's requirements that buildings be built with right angles and straight walls (figure 5-6).

Another great Shaker barn was the stone barn of Mount Lebanon's North Family (figure 5-7). Completed in 1858, this structure was among the largest of Shaker barns, measuring 193 feet long by 50 feet

5-5 The interior of Hancock's round barn shows the elaborate framing system required to support the circular wood loft and octagonal cupola. Numerous windows flood the interior with light.

5-6 An arch in the round barn shows the Hancock brethren to have been master stone masons.

5-7 A 1931 photograph of the south side of the Mount Lebanon, New York, North Family cow barn reveals the complex layout of the structure, which included extensive wagon sheds. Built into the hillside, the barn has several entrances at different levels. (Historic American Buildings Survey, Collection of the Library of Congress, Prints and Photographs Division.)

wide. Built into a steep hillside, the siting of the barn allowed vehicular access to three of its four levels. The main entrance faced the road leading into the village. Other entrances opened onto the cow yard to the south of the structure. Later addi-

tions off the south side accommodated cattle and farm equipment. The building functioned in much the same way that other barns did, using gravity to save labor in feeding cows on lower levels. Although the barn is less innovative than the round barn in terms of form, the scale of the building marks it as a unique structure. In the early 1970s the barn was destroyed by arson. Only the massive stone walls remain, a testament to the effort the Shakers put forth in their development of new and more enduring ways to build (figure 5-8).

The Hancock Shakers experimented with yet another barn form in the early twentieth century. After a wood-frame horse, cow, and hay barn burned down after being struck by lightning in 1910, the Shakers decided to build a structure better able to withstand fire. The solution was a rectangular barn set on a stone foundation, with the lower two stories made of poured concrete (figure 5-9). The upper two stories, framed and covered with planks of wood, were then coated with stucco to give the barn a uniform appearance. Slate tiles covered the roof, a final guard against fire (figure 5-10). The building still stands in stark contrast to the earlier round barn nearby. Whereas the Shakers still supervised construction of the newer barn, they no longer had the manpower to build it themselves.

Tobacco Barns

In addition to the barns used to shelter livestock and store hay, many Shaker villages had other kinds of barns. A common feature of the Pleasant Hill, Kentucky, village was the tobacco barn (figure 5-1, page 88). Nearly every Kentucky farmer grew tobacco, even if it was not his main cash crop. The

5-8 The ruins of the North Family barn at Mount Lebanon reveal the monolithic solidity of Shaker architecture. An arsonist destroyed the building in the early 1970s.

Pleasant Hill Shakers devoted some of their land to the growth of tobacco, though when they began to do so is unclear. Certainly they were growing it in the first half of the nineteenth century. Even though smoking, and the consumption of other stimulants, was banned by the Mount Lebanon ministry in 1841, Shakers at Pleasant Hill and at other communities continued to smoke pipes and take snuff. In the late nineteenth century the trustees at Pleasant Hill acquired a license to sell tobacco to visitors who stayed in the trustees' office. In 1914, only eight years before the community's closing, the

5-9 In 1910 the Church Family Shakers at Hancock hired workers to construct a fire-resistant barn made of concrete and wood covered with plaster. The barn, one of the last built at a Shaker village, illustrates the Shakers' willingness to try new building forms and techniques to create safer and more efficient structures.

5-10 Ongoing additions until 1939 enlarged Hancock's 1910 barn. This rooftop ventilator with a weathervane was probably purchased from the outside world.

Shakers at South Union agreed to allow a tenant farmer to grow tobacco on their land. The barns that remain today at Pleasant Hill, with their movable exterior siding, are typical of the tobacco barn form used in the bluegrass region of Kentucky.

Granaries

Granaries were another significant agricultural building type. Like barns, many of these structures no longer stand. Those that remain, however, point to the importance of grain as a food source for the Shakers (figure 5-11). The North Family's granary at Mount Lebanon holds a prominent position in the cluster of buildings at the north end of the village. The 2½-story wood-frame building stands between the remains of the family's stone barn and the laundry and dwelling, a good location for distributing grain to the various dwelling houses and barns in the family (figure 5-12). An enclosed chute tower juts out of the east wall of the granary.

Stables and Sheds

Although they attracted much less attention than barns, stables and sheds played an important role in both the agricultural and industrial production of Shaker communities. At times the Shakers seem to have used the words "stable" and "shed" almost interchangeably. Usually "stable" implied a

5-11 Whitewater, Ohio's grain barn (1875) is now deteriorated. The cupolas provided ventilation.

more substantial building for housing horses, whereas, "shed" typically indicated a smaller structure housing only a few horses, wagons, or equipment (figure 5-13). However, the word shed is often used on Shaker plans to indicate a large structure for sheltering horses. A typical shed form in the New England communities was a rectangular frame structure open on one long side, with a shed roof supported by roughly hewn square granite columns (figure 5-14). Every family within a

5-13 The Church Family's horse barn (1819) at Canterbury, New Hampshire, stabled horses for visitors and trustees.

5-12 The Mount Lebanon North Family's granary provided grain storage. A gabled chute tower juts out from the structure.

Shaker village had a stable for its horses. In addition, the trustees and the ministry had separate stables for their own teams of horses. Thus, small stables stood behind or next to the office and the ministry shop.

Although water provided power for many tasks, sometimes the Shakers attached sheds to workshops if horsepower was needed to execute a specific task. The cooper's shop at Union Village is one such example. During Isaac N. Youngs's visit to the community in 1834, he noted with great interest the horse shed connected to the Center Family's cooper's shop. At this family nearly all the barrel-making was done with machinery driven by horses walking on an inclined wheel.[20]

Unfortunately, the majority of Shaker stables and sheds have been destroyed. With the advent of the car and the departure of the Shakers from most

of their villages in the late nineteenth and early twentieth centuries, these humble structures were destroyed or neglected. Understandably, early preservation efforts focused first on the larger and more significant Shaker structures, leaving lesser-known buildings to decay and destruction.

Nevertheless, one horse stable has been saved and recently reconstructed at Pleasant Hill. Built in 1866, the stable was constructed in the manner of wood-frame barns, with large timbers erected in bays and mortised and tenoned to form solid joints. The structure, located along the road leading to the Shakers' landing by the Kentucky River, housed horses which provided transportation between the river and the Shaker village. The survival of this large stable serves as a reminder of the Shaker villages' dependence on horses for transportation and trade until the railroad replaced all but local horse travel. The society sold many of its goods, particularly seeds, by sending brothers on horseback on sales trips that lasted for several weeks. As the railroad pushed its way into the countryside, Shaker villages, like other villages, gradually relied more on trains to ship goods, and horse stables and sheds became less central.

As work buildings, barns, stables, and sheds reflected the agricultural side of Shaker villages. Their importance in the health of the Shaker economy encouraged Shaker builders to experiment with architectural forms in order to maximize efficiency. While a majority of the buildings have succumbed to fire, demolition, or ruin, some of the most distinctive have survived. Innovative barns, such as Hancock's round barn, testify to the significance of architectural experimentation in the life of the sect.

5-14 The North Family wagon shed (ca. 1860) at Mount Lebanon may have been constructed as a garden house and later converted. At one time, the shed had a large wood ramp that could be let down from the lower-level ceiling to provide access to the upper level.

6 Workshops and Mills

Perfection Through Labor

AS AGRICULTURAL AND manufacturing communities, the Shakers depended on workshops and mills for the economic well-being of the sect. Within these buildings the Shakers produced goods both for their own communities and for sale to the outside world. The term "shop" covered many of the buildings in a village—ministry shops, blacksmith shops, tan houses, cooper's shops, spinning shops, and broom shops. "Mills" encompassed structures such as grist mills, oil mills, and saw mills. Together, these building types represented the industrial nature of their community, a necessary element of the sect's plan to create a perfect society.

6-1 Herb storage and packing room, laundry building, Sabbathday Lake. The Shakers in Maine continue to produce herbs and seeds for sale to the world in much the same way earlier Shakers had, though on a smaller scale.

Shaker Manufacturing and Water Power

The robustness of the Shaker economy in the late eighteenth and nineteenth centuries relied upon the variety of tasks that each village could perform and goods it could produce. Extensive water systems permitted such diversity by providing the power for the Shakers to process large quantities of lumber, leather, and fabric. The Shakers built aqueducts and canals to bring water from nearby rivers or lakes into their shops and dwellings (figure 6-2). Many workshops, particularly in the eastern communities, were powered by large wheels located in narrow stone-lined chambers sunk below the buildings. Water, traveling through underground pipes, turned the wheels that powered machinery in the buildings above. By combining the resources of hundreds of individuals to construct these systems, the Shakers fostered industrial development in the

6-2 The remains of this stone dam at Mount Lebanon, New York, serve as a reminder of the extensive water-power systems at nineteenth-century Shaker villages. The dam formed the north wall of the mill pond. Water traveled from the pond to the mill's water wheel via a cast-iron drop flume.

countryside at a time when it was rarely seen in rural settings (except in growing mill towns such as Lowell, Massachusetts). This aspect of the Shakers is often ignored by historians who claim that the group was strictly agricultural. Water was also used extensively in the West, but in many cases small, isolated shops there relied on horses to power single pieces of machinery.

Brethren's and Sisters' Shops

Each village had a brethren's shop and a sisters' shop in accordance with the Millennial Laws which said that brethren and sisters could not work together. Brethren's shops usually included areas for tailoring (only brothers made clothes for brothers, while sisters made clothes for sisters, though sisters generally did the mending for all members), light carpentry, and shoemaking (figure 6-3). Sisters' shops housed tasks such as spinning and weaving, bonnet-making, and rug-making (figures 6-4 and 6-5). However, brethren's and sisters' shops were sometimes the sites of heavy manufacturing, too. For this reason, they were often built of brick or stone so that they could withstand the repeated movements of turning gears and belts that drove lathes, saws, and other tools (figures 6-6 and 6-7). The possibility of fire—a danger in places where the Shakers used wood-burning stoves or later steam engines, boilers, and machinery running at high speeds and temperatures—also encouraged the use of brick and stone.

Ministry Shops

The ministry shop of each village provided work space for the ministry elders and eldresses. Although the ministry provided spiritual leadership for the community, its members also

6-3   The East Family brethren's shop (1845) and cooper's shop (moved 1847) at Pleasant Hill, Kentucky, testify to the specialization of labor at Shaker villages. In the brick brethren's shop, brothers printed labels for seed and herb packages and made broom handles. In the cooper's shop, brothers produced barrels, pails, and similar wooden containers.

6-4 The Church Family dairy and weave shop (1795; enlarged ca. 1820) at Hancock, Massachusetts, was originally built as a dairy, where the sisters made cheese and other milk products. After 1820 the Shakers added a loft which provided space for the sisters to weave fabric.

performed physical labor to set an example of industry for the other Shakers. In this way they fulfilled Mother Ann's well-known proverb: "Put your hands to work and your hearts to God." Because they lived apart from the rest of the community in the meeting house, the ministry also worked in their own building. The ministry shop stood next to the meeting house in each community (figure 6-8). This location not only made getting to the shop more convenient for the ministry, but it also contrasted the temporal aspects of the ministry's leadership, embodied in the shop, with its spiritual aspects, represented in the meeting house.

Ministry shops do not appear in Shaker villages until the late 1820s and early 1830s. Charles F. Priest's plan of the Church Family at Harvard, drawn in 1833, shows a tiny ministry shop, only 1½ stories tall, standing between the meeting house and the sisters' shop.[21] An 1838 map of the Church Family at Watervliet, New York, shows a slightly larger ministry shop of two by two bays and 2½ stories.[22] By the 1830s, many villages had modest ministry shops of brick or wood, standing 2½ stories high with gable roofs and simple central hall plans with four rooms on the first floor and four rooms above (figure 6-9). The first floors had a meeting room, a kitchen, and a dining room. (However, the ministry sometimes had its own dining room within the family's main dwelling house, as is the case at Pleasant Hill; figure 6-10.) The ministry shops' other rooms provided work space, and later retiring rooms, for the two elders and two eldresses (figure 6-11). Ministry shops always had only one front entrance that both elders and eldresses used. This arrangement demonstrated the spiritual sanctity and physical control exhibited by the ministry. Usually, though not always, these Shakers were elderly and performed light tasks that could be done indoors. Some elders helped build buildings and made furniture and other objects; eldresses made baskets or sewed. The elders and eldresses spent more time on disseminating spiritual doctrine, correspondence with other communities, and keeping journals.

Originally the ministry shop was designed to provide only a work place for the ministry, but later it also became their home. After the Great Fire of 1875 at Mount Lebanon, the Church Family erected a new ministry shop along with a new dwelling house. The brick ministry shop still stands today, a small, elegant structure with stone window sills and arched lintels. It is a miniature version of the large dwelling house next to it, sharing the Great House's worldliness. Built from 1876 to

1878, the ministry shop provided more comfortable accommodations for the ministry than the older meeting house (figure 6-12). The Shakers included a heating system and hot and cold running water throughout the shop, whereas in the meeting house the ministry had relied on wood-burning stoves. By moving out of the meeting house, the Mount Lebanon ministry, as the head Shaker ministry, marked a significant shift in Shakerism toward secularization. These Shakers, who were supposed to lead the way toward spiritual perfection and salvation, had forsaken the most sacred building of the village as their home and, instead, adopted the ministry shop with its temporal associations.

Workshops

In addition to the brethren's and sisters' shops and the ministry shop, many villages built other workshops for specialized tasks, depending on the type or amount of local production. While the

6-5   The Pleasant Hill East Family sisters' shop (1855), divided into two sections by a central hall, provided work space for the sisters to spin thread and weave cloth. The sisters also made a variety of other goods here which they sold to the world, such as baskets, palm-leaf bonnets, and silk scarves.

collection of shops varied from village to village, most communities had tan houses, blacksmith's shops, carpentry shops, tin shops, seed shops, and herb shops (figures 6-13 and 6-14). In tan houses brothers produced leather to make shoes, saddles, bridles and other goods for the community. Because of the messy nature of cleaning and then tanning the hides in vats of brine, tan houses were often located away from the main road, down-

stream from the rest of the village, where the cleaning process could be done easily and safely. Tan houses can still be seen at Mount Lebanon, Hancock, and Pleasant Hill (figures 6-15 and 6-16).

The presence of tin shops, cooper's shops, and blacksmith's shops also attests to the self-sufficiency of the large Shaker villages such as Mount Lebanon, Union Village, and Pleasant Hill during their peak years in the 1830s and 1840s. However, smaller villages often had trouble finding enough Shaker labor to carry out all the tasks required to meet the communities' needs. At the tiny village of Watervliet, Ohio, hired men ran the mill, the tannery, and the wagon shop. These three men and their families lived near their work places in their own houses that the Shakers built for them on Shaker land. Although the Mount Lebanon ministry wished to lessen the dependence on hired help, the lack of able-bodied men required smaller Shaker villages to look outside their communities for labor even in their early years. This problem became more significant as the years passed and the Shakers lost more and more men. Gradually, hired men provided most, if not all, of the labor at every Shaker village. As this population increased, many villages constructed "Hired Men's Houses" for these workers.

As agricultural communities, Shaker villages were concerned with the production of seeds for sowing their fields. They grew their own seeds to ensure high-quality crops. Many villages also sold seeds to the world, bringing a great deal of money to the communities each year due to the Shakers' outstanding reputation for quality. As this industry grew, the Shakers built seed shops or converted old buildings which had outlasted their original

6-6 The sturdy brick North Family brethren's shop (1829) at Mount Lebanon housed many water-powered machines, such as lathes, drills, and saws. It also served as the laundry until the North Family moved operations to another building. Later the Shakers ran a print shop, seed shop, and shoemaker's shop in the building. After 1900, the Shakers housed hired workers on the upper floors.

6-7   Like the brick shop at Mount Lebanon, the stone walls of the machine shop (1849) at Enfield, New Hampshire, provided solid support for water-powered and, later, engine-driven machinery. Numerous windows throughout the building admitted plenty of natural light by which the brothers worked.

6-8 The simple wood-frame ministry shop (1820) at Pleasant Hill, Kentucky, provided first work space and then living quarters for the ministry. The single entrance and central hall plan were typical features of this building type. The trustees' office stands to the left, the meeting house to the right.

purposes. For instance, the first meeting house at Mount Lebanon became the Church Family's seed shop in 1839. The production of medicinal herbs also brought income to the villages. Many villages built large wood-frame still shops and herb shops with elaborate equipment for distilling herbs to produce a variety of tonics. On his three-day visit to Mount Lebanon in August 1856, the journalist Benson J. Lossing marveled at the seed, herb, and medicinal extract operations. He noted that many sisters worked under brothers who managed the various shops in a clean, efficient manner. Everywhere, he said, "perfect order and neatness prevail."[23] Both the seed and herb industries spawned secondary tasks, including the printing of labels and seed packets, which were usually performed in the same or nearby buildings. The seed and herb industry continues today on a small scale at Sabbathday Lake (figure 6-1, page 102).

6-9 Ministry shop (1839; enlarged 1875), Sabbathday Lake, Maine. These shops, as the work places of the ministry, always stood next to the meeting houses, where they resided. The setting allowed the elders and eldresses to move back and forth between the two buildings without having to meet other members of the community, interaction forbidden by the Millennial Laws.

The Commercialization of Shaker Goods

Other workshops emerged in the second half of the nineteenth century as certain Shaker goods, such as brooms, chairs, cloaks, and fancy goods, became extremely popular in the outside world. The production of Shaker brooms accelerated after the Civil War. The Shakers had always made brooms for their own use, but they found that they could sell many more. Demand in Kentucky and Ohio was so high that Pleasant Hill converted its carpenter shop into a broom shop in 1870. This transformation allowed the Pleasant Hill Shakers to meet the demand for their brooms, but it also meant they had to purchase more wood products ready-made from the world. In 1876 Whitewater built its own broom shop. The sale of brooms soon became the community's major source of income. Compared to many other Shaker structures, the L-shaped building is poorly put together; perhaps the Whitewater Shakers were in such a hurry to build it and get their broom industry going that they neglected to square the walls. From 1876 to the end of the century this small community produced thousands of brooms each year.

The production and sale of Shaker chairs evolved in a similar way. Although the Shakers had

6-10 The ministry at Pleasant Hill took meals in their own dining room attached to the rear of the Center Family dwelling house. Shaker law required the ministry to live separately from other Shakers to preserve their spiritual purity.

sold their chairs to the world as early as the late eighteenth century, they increased production in the 1870s because of the growing popularity of Shaker crafts. The South Family at Mount Lebanon built its chair factory in 1872. The large, ungainly, wood-frame structure stands 3½ stories tall, its walls sheathed with vertical boards and battens. The interior contained machine-powered saws and lathes that could turn out pieces for chairs in a few hours. Robert Wagan, of Mount Lebanon's South Family, proved to be a driving force behind the growing demand for Shaker chairs. On his own initiative, he exhibited the chairs at the 1876 Centennial Exposition in Philadelphia, where they won a medal and received national, even international, attention. In addition, Wagan heavily advertised the chairs through the Shakers' own catalogs and announcements in newspapers. As a result, the

6-11 Ministry shop (1874), Hancock, Massachusetts. Ministry shops provided space for the elders and eldresses to perform light tasks such as keeping journals or making baskets.

South Family's chair production increased to satisfy demand. In December 1879, a South Family sister noted that there was "a great demand for chairs & cushions to meet the holidays."[24] In 1881 the craze for Shaker chairs had increased even more, "great Orders for chairs cannot make fast enough."[25] The South Family continued to produce chairs for other Mount Lebanon families, but again, the priority placed on the manufacture of goods for the world, rather than those for the community, prevailed. The need to maintain a steady level of production required that men and women work together, and so the long-held rule mandating separation collapsed under the desire to maintain a high standard of living.

As the Shakers put more labor and resources into the manufacture of goods for sale to the world, they drew available labor from tasks such as carpentry, tailoring, and shoemaking. Instead of making furniture, clothing, and shoes for themselves, the Shakers had to purchase them ready-made from stores. Eventually, the sect's members bought most of their products from the outside, making the maintenance of their own separate identity increasingly difficult. In this way, the Shaker communities served as microcosms of the nineteenth-century rural world.

Mills

Like workshops, mills were an integral part of the Shaker economy. One of the earliest structures erected at Mount Lebanon, after the meeting house and the first dwelling houses, was the grist mill. The difficulty of erecting a mill and the building's functional importance required the skills of a talented builder. Moses Johnson, the builder of all the

6-12 Elder Giles B. Avery designed the ministry shop (1876-78) at Mount Lebanon, New York, to replace the shop burned in the Great Fire of 1875. The arched lintels over the windows and the stone door surround lend a worldly air to the structure. Upon completion of the shop, the ministry moved out of the meeting house to reside in the new building.

early meeting houses in the East, stayed on to oversee the construction of the Church Family's grist mill, about 1790, before leaving Mount Lebanon to supervise the building of the meeting houses at other villages.

Because of the large quantity of grain that needed to be processed, Shaker grist mills were often huge structures. The most solid ones were constructed of stone, usually standing three or four stories high and built into the side of a hill near a race so that water could turn the gears, as in conventional mills. North Union's stone grist mill had three stone runs and its height of more than 50 feet created a 40-to-54-foot drop that

6-13 Blacksmith shop, Church Family tan house (1835), Hancock. The Shakers produced iron goods for themselves and for sale to the world until the twentieth century. As the number of male Shakers declined, however, the Shakers turned to the outside world for ironwork and other metalware.

6-14 Cabinetry shop, Church Family tan house, Hancock. With a wide range of carpentry tools, skilled Shaker brothers constructed cabinets and architectural elements.

6-15 The Church Family erected their large tan house (1834) at Mount Lebanon in response to the family's growing demand for leather goods. The community's extensive water system provided power to run machinery throughout the building.

provided ample water power. The Shakers' combined resources permitted them to build what were often the first mills in developing rural areas. Not only did the mills grind Shaker grain, they also provided additional income by grinding the grain of neighboring farmers.

In the East, grist mills were generally integrated into each family's group of buildings. However, at some of the Shaker villages in Ohio and Kentucky, separate mill areas, such as the "Grist Mill Family" at Union Village, or the "Mill Family" at Pleasant Hill, served all the communities' milling needs. These areas encompassed the grist mill, saw mill, oil mill, and carding machine. Both the Ohio and Kentucky Shakers grew flax from which they pressed linseed oil. In addition, both Union Village and Pleasant Hill produced large quantities of linen textiles from the flax, greatly facilitated by water-powered carding machines. By the 1820s, the Shakers at Union Village had constructed an extensive system of four mill ponds with dams along Shaker Creek to power three saw mills, a grist mill, an oil mill, and a fulling (cloth-processing) mill. Sometimes these projects significantly altered the landscape: for example, the mill pond at the Grist Mill Family encompassed twenty-one acres.

Like the grist mills, Shaker saw mills provided the means to process lumber for the Shakers' own building and carpentry projects as well as bringing in money from nearby non-Shakers who needed lumber sawn. Every village had at least one sawmill; larger villages often had more. Until the late nineteenth century, the Shakers brought timber from their own forests as far away as Michigan, and sawed and planed it in their own mills. Without the capacity to produce their own building lumber, the Shakers would have had to spend more money on the many ongoing construction projects for dwellings, shops, and other buildings. The number and type of workshops could vary greatly from one village to another. A ca. 1820 map of Hancock shows a variety of shops. In addition to the ones mentioned above, Hancock also had a machine shop, a clothier's shop, and a hatter's shop. The maps of western Shaker villages that Isaac N. Youngs drew in the summer of 1834 attest to the wide range of shops of various sizes present at these communities.[26]

The Shaker Work Ethic

Shaker maps and views and historic photographs reveal the number and diversity of Shaker workshops. As a separatist Protestant sect, Shakerism adopted many beliefs espoused by similar groups that had come before them, including the Quakers and the Methodists. One of these was that constant labor prevented idleness. By filling the days from dawn to dusk with work, the Shakers used their time productively. They believed that labor worked a positive influence on individuals, in part by keeping them too busy to think about physical needs. In a practical sense, the prosperity of each village depended on the labor of all capable hands for the well-being of the entire community.

As the Shakers grew to rely more on hired help, they lost hold of this work ethic. Often hired help and their families lived with the Shakers, bringing their worldly ways into the community and in direct contact with the brothers and sisters. Furthermore, as the majority of Shakers grew older, they became accustomed to working less and relying more on the labor provided by hired hands. This dependence on people of the world no doubt contributed to the decline of Shakerism in the late nineteenth century by de-emphasizing the significance of work as part of the Shaker religion.

Over the years, many workshops and mills, no longer in use, were torn down or abandoned and left to decay. Their sites, often on the outskirts of the villages, were the first land to be sold off by the Shakers as their communities lost members. Today, most of the preserved Shaker villages have only a few of the dozens of shops that animated every

6-16 Like the Mount Lebanon tan house, the Church Family tan house (1835) at Hancock, Massachusetts, is also wood-frame set on a stone foundation. Such construction provided a sturdy building capable of withstanding the movement of machinery used in the tanning process. The Shakers used the entire building for tanning until around 1875, when they converted parts of it into a blacksmith shop (on the ground floor) and a cabinetry shop (on the second floor; see figures 6-13 and 6-14).

community. In addition, the water systems that powered many of the shops and mills have long since been dismantled or destroyed. Thus, the visitor is left with neither a sense of the vast network of water power that made Shaker villages like miniature versions of early New England mill towns nor of the Shaker efforts to transform their environments into prosperous communities.

Instead, these vestigial villages convey the impression that the communities were mostly pastoral, agrarian societies. Nineteenth-century descriptions and photographs attest, however, to the industrial aspect of Shaker society. Rather than the peaceful, almost park-like places they now are, Shaker communities of the nineteenth century were noisy, active centers of production and commerce.

7 Laundry Buildings

Perfection through Cleanliness

ALTHOUGH LAUNDRY BUILDINGS are technically workshops, they are considered as a separate building type here because of their unique function in Shaker communities. In many ways laundry buildings (or "wash houses" as they are also called) express better than any other Shaker building the Believers' desire for order and cleanliness. Nearly every family had its own laundry where the "laundry sisters" washed, dried, and ironed clothes and other textiles for the entire family. With the removal of the laundry tasks from the dwelling houses, the Shakers were able to make such chores more efficient by designing buildings best suited to the maintenance of clothing.

7-1 Vents along the north and east sides of the Mount Lebanon, New York, North Family laundry building and wood shed (ca. 1854) permitted air circulation for wood stored inside. The laundry section stood at the other end. The second and third floors provided space for seed drying and packaging.

Early Laundry Buildings

In the eastern communities these buildings number among the earliest structures built. Most of the laundry buildings were wood, though in later years the Shakers also built brick wash houses. The Canterbury Shakers erected their laundry in 1795 and continued to enlarge it in the nineteenth century (figure 7-2). Today, the structure is characterized by a variety of additions with different roof shapes and an awkward floor plan—the result of poorly planned and clumsily built accretions. As it now stands, Canterbury's laundry building is a 2¹/₂-story structure with a medium-pitch gable roof. Off the north side of the original wood-frame building is an addition with a brick first story and two wood-frame upper stories. Numerous windows allow light into the second floor. Eventually, most eastern laundry shops evolved into solid, wood-frame structures built to withstand the constant motion of belts and gears that powered the large washing machines and wringers.

Because of their function, laundry buildings were usually not attractive structures. Often they were connected to other buildings or they provided space for tasks other than washing and drying clothes. Thus, a laundry might also serve as a workshop or a wood house. They were amorphous buildings receiving additions or new tasks as the family's needs changed. For example, the Hancock Church Family's laundry is important in that it shows how organic and imperfect some Shaker buildings could be (figure 7-3). The structure seems to have been originally built around 1790 as a machine shop. Sunk below the east end of the building is a chamber that housed a waterwheel to provide power for the machinery. The first floor of

7-2 The irregular shape of the Canterbury, New Hampshire, Church Family laundry (1795) is a result of the various nineteenth-century additions made to the structure. The original part of the building stands to the left.

7-3   Church Family laundry building and machine shop (ca. 1790; additions until 1870), Hancock, Massachusetts. The different types of wood siding and the windows crowding the roofline emphasize the awkward form of this building—the result of ill-planned additions. Built first as a machine shop, the building later accommodated the sisters' laundry as well.

7-4 The boxy South Family laundry building (1851) at Mount Lebanon, New York, features an arched, recessed entrance, unusual in Shaker architecture. The structure served a dual purpose as the sisters' laundry and workshop, bringing numerous tasks under one roof for efficiency and convenience.

the building was used as a sawmill. Later, the Shakers converted the west end into a laundry shop. Two additions, neither aligned with the main part of the laundry building, provided extra work space along the south side. In addition, as machinery was added to the shop, random framing was built to support it, but the builders paid little attention to how the framing fit in with the original fabric of the structure.[27] From an examination of this building and other wash houses, it is clear that the Shakers did not always conceive their buildings as permanent structures, nor did they attempt to make every one of them perfect.

Nineteenth-Century Laundry Buildings in the East

Another example of the flexibility of laundry buildings is the 1851 laundry at Mount Lebanon's South Family that also functioned as the sisters' workshop (figure 7-4). The laundry tasks took place on the lower levels while other chores, such as weaving and sewing, were performed on the upper floors of the 3½-story structure. The laundry's cellar and first floor were built of stone, while the upper levels were of wood-frame construction. The building's masonry entrance arch covering the front door is unique in Shaker architecture and suggests experimentation on the part of the builders, though there is no discussion of this design feature in Shaker records. Later, the Shakers built a wood catwalk to link the laundry to the South Family's chair shop next door. This bridge, spanning 30 feet, exited the laundry from the third floor and entered the chair shop on the second floor, allowing more convenient access for the sis-

7-5 Probably the grandest laundry at any Shaker village, the brick Center Family laundry building (1854) at South Union, Kentucky, has a symmetrical, tripartite facade. Stone lintels cap the windows and doors, giving the structure the appearance of a Shaker dwelling rather than a laundry building.

ters between the two buildings. By building this bridge, the Shakers recognized the growing role women were playing in the commercial enterprises of the family.

The laundry at Mount Lebanon's North Family presents another example of a laundry building type (figure 7-1). In addition to the laundry, this shop included a wood shed. The Shakers chose to build the entire structure of wood despite the danger of fire—a real threat considering the proximity of so much flammable material near rooms where washing, drying, and ironing clothes required a great amount of heat from wood-burning stoves (or, later, boilers). The North Family Shakers provided ventilation through a series of vents running around the north end of the building where wood was stored. The experiment seems to have worked, as the building is still standing today.

7-6   The East Family laundry building at Pleasant Hill, Kentucky, contains large iron cauldrons and wood hoists used to wash and then lift wet clothes.

Nineteenth-Century Laundry Buildings in the West

Few laundry buildings remain in the western communities, and nearly all of these are brick. The exceptions are the West and East Family laundries at Pleasant Hill. Archival records, too, indicate that wash houses were often built of brick in these communities, again pointing to the preference for brick over wood in the West. These large laundry buildings were constructed later in the history of the western communities than in the eastern communities, suggesting that before then, the Shakers did their laundry in other buildings such as the sisters' workshops. Those laundry buildings that remain standing were, for the most part, con-structed in the 1840s and 1850s—Pleasant Hill: East Family, wood-frame, 1825 (addition 1849), West Family, wood-frame, 1842; Whitewater: brick, 1853; South Union: brick, 1854 (figure 7-5). These structures seem to have been exclusively devoted to laundry tasks and related chores such as making soap, weaving, and spinning, whereas many of the laundries in the eastern communities, such as those at Enfield, New Hampshire, contin-ued to house unrelated tasks, such as laundry and dairy work.

The later laundry buildings of the western com-munities also seem to have been better planned than those in the East. The three-story brick laun-dry at South Union has a symmetrical facade with evenly spaced doors and windows (figure 7-5).

The walls, pierced with many windows, reveal the Shakers' concern with light and ventilation, particularly in a building where the sisters performed heavy tasks. Whitewater's 2½-story laundry also follows a symmetrical arrangement of windows and doors. Both buildings, though constructed in the 1850s, continue to reflect the Shakers' taste for the Federal style, clearly anachronistic by this time.

The presence of laundry buildings set the Shakers apart from their non-Shaker neighbors in terms of the mechanization of clothing maintenance. Until the 1870s and 1880s, water powered most Shaker machinery, including washing machines. During these decades, the Shakers switched to steam as a more efficient power source. However, the North Family Shakers at Mount Lebanon continued to use a Backus 1872 turbine water motor at their laundry building and wood shed into the twentieth century. Though it is questionable whether the Shakers actually invented the washing machine (as many historians have suggested), they did make many advances in this technology, even patenting a machine that they sold to large hotels. The only such machine left can be found at the Shaker Museum in Old Chatham, New York.

7-7 Before the Shakers mechanized their laundry process, they used large tubs and wood beaters to clean clothes, as seen in the Hancock, Massachusetts, Church Family laundry building and machine shop.

Maintenance of Clothing and Textiles

Despite the presence of machines, laundry chores were labor intensive. After washing the clothes in large vats or troughs, the sisters put them onto dumbwaiters that raised the damp loads to the upper floor where the drying racks stood (figures 7-6, 7-7, and 7-8). Like the washing machines, these racks were adaptations of racks used "in the world." In the latter part of the nineteenth century such racks were built into hotels and mansions (including the Vanderbilt estate of Biltmore in Asheville, North Carolina, where they can still be seen). These racks, which ran from the floor to the ceiling, could be pulled out of the drying room on runners so that wet clothes could be hung on them. The sisters then pushed the racks back into the drying room, where hot air from stoves circulated through the clothes. After the garments dried, the sisters either ironed them, using hot irons from special stoves with heating racks, or

7-8 Drying room, North Family laundry building, Mount Lebanon. The Shakers used wood racks in heated rooms to dry their clothing. These racks moved in and out of the drying room on metal rails in the floor.

folded them and placed them in presses for about a week (figure 7-9).

The Shakers kept track of all their clothing and other textiles by marking each article with a code that noted the building and the room from which the article came. Napkins and table cloths from the dwelling house dining room would be marked as such. An article of clothing could likewise be returned to its specific retiring room. Because of the communal nature of all property, clothing did not technically belong to individuals, although specific items of clothing were made to fit a particular body. The numbered bins in the washing room at Canterbury, as well as the numbered bins and baskets in which clothing would be placed after it was ironed and folded, demonstrate the laundry-sorting system in operation there.

Not only does the attention paid to laundry reveal the order that pervaded Shaker life, but it also indicates the strong desire for physical cleanliness that was a part of the Shakers' religious beliefs. For the Shakers, keeping things neat and clean showed respect for God, since dirt was considered a sign of the devil. During a period of religious revivals in the late 1830s and 1840s called "Mother Ann's Work," the Shakers instituted a ceremony called the Sweeping Gift. Once a year the brothers and sisters marched through all the buildings of the village sweeping out evil with imaginary brooms. This custom lasted until the revivals ended in the late 1840s.

Although the desire for cleanliness is strongly associated with the Shakers, such a concern also existed in the outside world. Contemporary prescriptive books such as Catharine Beecher's *A Treatise on Domestic Economy, for the use of young ladies at home, and at school* (1841) discuss at great length the importance of keeping a clean and well-ventilated house to maintain health.[28] While the Shakers may have been aware of such literature, many of their rules concerning cleanliness came out of a wish for spiritual purity, as well. In a large community with hundreds of inhabitants, cleanliness in the yards, the water supply, and inside buildings was critical to the health of the community. By making the pursuit of cleanliness a religious doctrine, the Shakers internalized it and ensured its observance within the community.

7-9 Ironing room, Church Family laundry building and machine shop, Hancock. The Shakers designed large coal-burning stoves with shelves to heat dozens of flat irons. As in other Shaker buildings, many windows enabled sisters to work with plenty of light.

8 School Houses

Shaping Shakers Through Education

THE PRESENCE OF SCHOOL HOUSES bears witness to the Shaker emphasis on education. Children attended school until the age of sixteen for boys and fourteen for girls, at which time they moved to the main dwellings to live with the adults and assumed daily chores. Boys and girls were taught separately and at different times of the year; the boys during the winter, when agricultural tasks were few, and the girls during the summer. Sometimes the brothers and sisters who served as the caretakers of the boys and girls also worked as school teachers. However, many villages assigned well-educated Shakers to this task.

8-1 Church Family school house (ca. 1820; 1976 reconstruction), Hancock, Massachusetts. The teacher's desk, set on an elevated platform before the students' desks, was a common feature in both Shaker and non-Shaker schools.

Shaker Education

The variety of subjects taught reveals that the Shakers provided a well-rounded curriculum. The Millennial Laws specified the following topics: "Spelling, Reading, Writing, Composition, English Grammar, Arithmetic, Mensuration [geometrical measurement], The Science of Agriculture, Agricultural Chemistry, a small portion of History and Geography, Architecture, Moral Science, Good Manners, and True Religion."[29] These courses prepared children to function within Shaker society as productive members of the community (figure 8-1).

The practice of providing children, boys and girls, with some formal education and a great deal of manual training predated the advent of public schools in most of the United States, though not in New England. Hancock seems to have been the first Shaker village to establish a school, doing so in

1791. In 1800 the town of Hancock designated it a separate school district. In 1808 the Shakers at Mount Lebanon permitted instruction in spelling and manners. In 1813–14 evening schools and afternoon classes were instituted there to teach spelling, reading, writing, and arithmetic. The Church Family at Mount Lebanon established a public school in 1817 with an expanded curricu-

lum. At the same time, Hancock's school also became public, opening to local non-Shaker children. Its school house, constructed circa 1820–30, was moved in the early twentieth century and is now a private home.

In 1821 Brother Seth Y. Wells, who had been an instructor in the public schools of Albany and at Hudson Academy in Hudson, New York, was

appointed as superintendent of the Shaker schools in the Mount Lebanon bishopric. He expanded the curriculum further and allowed the schools to be inspected by state officials. Under his stewardship, Shaker schools were opened to the children of the "world's people" and became eligible to receive public funding.

In the first decades of the nineteenth century, the Shakers conducted school in makeshift buildings. Initially, children were most likely taught in their dwellings. The first school house at Mount Lebanon's Church Family was actually the old meeting house, which had been replaced by a new structure in 1824. If school houses existed at all in the western communities, they were log cabins. A copy of Isaac N. Youngs's 1834 map of North Union, Ohio, shows that the first school house in the village provided the name for the family in which it stood—the "School Family." The sight of log cabins greatly interested Youngs, who had never seen them in the East: "Saw a number of the boys, & the grand log school house with a big dutch fireplace & a sort of ladder to go up the stairs!"[30]

Construction of Shaker School Houses

In 1839 the construction of a building designed specifically for use as a school house at Mount Lebanon signaled the new emphasis the Shakers were placing on education. The building still stands. It is a simple 2½-story wood-frame structure atop a first story of cut stone. The single front door leads into a large open school room with a kitchen at the south end. Another open school room occupies the second floor. In both rooms the teacher's desk stood on a raised platform before the students' desks. This arrangement can still be seen in the Canterbury School House (figure 8-2). The only details that set the structure apart as a Shaker building were the pegboards running along the walls in the rooms. These boards, flat moldings with wood pegs projecting from them, appeared in virtually all Shaker buildings and were used to hang up everything from clothing to candlesticks to chairs. The Shaker school layout follows the prescriptions of Horace Mann, the Secretary of the Board of Education for the state of Massachusetts. In the 1830s Mann published reports that included plans for school buildings that he believed would foster conditions for improved education. It is certainly possible that the Shakers knew of his ideas and incorporated them.

The example of the school house at Mount Lebanon led to the gradual construction of school buildings at other Shaker villages. Canterbury, New Hampshire, had one school house, built in 1823. The village's girls were taught in their own dwelling, the "Girls' House," also called the "Girls' School" (1810). Both these structures remain standing at Canterbury Shaker Village. The Canterbury school house reveals the Shakers' ingenuity in modifying old structures to make them newly useful rather than demolishing them. (figure 8-3) The Shakers jacked up the building a full story and constructed a new floor below, thereby

8-2 The Church Family school house (1823, enlarged 1863) at Canterbury, New Hampshire, contains desks made in the world. Shaker schools, under the authority of the local public school system, became increasingly worldly over the years as students from the outside outnumbered Shaker children.

8-3   Originally a one-story structure, the Canterbury school house gained an extra story
in 1863 when the Shakers jacked up the old building and built a new story beneath it.
This method enabled the Shakers to retain the original roof and foundation.

retaining the slate roof on the old building.

The Shakers continued to build school houses during the nineteenth century. Whitewater, Ohio, built a brick building 20 by 30 feet to accommodate its students. At smaller communities, the construction of school houses seems to have been a low priority. The community at Alfred, Maine, did not build its school house until 1861. With fewer resources and Shakers of school age, classes could be conducted inside the children's houses or in dwelling houses. However, the fact that even small villages built school houses indicates that education was considered an integral part of Shaker life (figure 8-4).

Worldly Influences

Despite the Shakers' goal to educate children as productive Shakers who would live out their lives within the sect, the quality of a Shaker education attracted children from the outside world. Because the Shakers accepted public funds and were inspected by state officials, they had to accept children from outside their communities. Of course this interaction made it difficult to maintain the isolation of Shaker children from the world. Shaker children came to the sect when their parents converted, when their parents indentured them to the Shakers for a number of years, or when the Shakers adopted them as orphans. When Shaker children reached adulthood, most of them left the society, having never entered it by choice. As the communities shrank, the declining number of children required additional changes in the way the Shakers ran their schools. In many cases, the Shakers taught more children from outside the village than from within it. Another major change involved the teaching of boys and girls together. For example, in 1880 South Union, Kentucky, began coeducational classes.

8-4 Sabbathday Lake's one-room school house (1880) served as a school for Shakers and non-Shakers until 1950. It now functions as the Shaker community's library.

Nevertheless, many Shaker schools continued to run well into the twentieth century. The Watervliet, New York, Shaker School District No. 14 survived until the 1920s. According to Dorothy M. Filley, in its last years, two girls raised by the Shakers as well as six boys and girls, the children of tenant farmers, attended the school.[31] As villages closed, their schools were consolidated with other districts.

Although the earliest Shakers had considered formal education to be harmful to the growth of faith, Shaker schools served an important function after the eighteenth century. Perhaps a Shaker education, more than other aspects of Shakerism, had the greatest impact on young members of the sect in the nineteenth and early twentieth centuries. During this period the Shakers educated hundreds of children, Shaker and non-Shaker alike. Although their intention was to shape children into good Shakers, they often gave their graduates the education and the vocational skills needed to succeed in the outside world as well.

9 Infirmaries

Healing the Sick

INFIRMARIES, ALSO KNOWN AS "nurse's shops," were another type of specialized structure that appeared in the nineteenth century. Their genesis was due in part to the growing population of aged Shakers and in part to the Shakers' tendency to categorize members, the infirmary allowed the physical removal of sick members from the rest of the family. Such separation kept ill, non-working Shakers from the working brothers and sisters. The infirmary provided a quiet place for members to recover (as opposed to the dwelling house, which was full of activity from the time the Believers rose before dawn to the time they retired to bed, around

9:00 p.m.). In addition, the infirmary helped prevent contagious diseases from spreading by isolating sick Shakers (figure 9-2).

Early "Sick Houses"

Early nineteenth-century maps of Shaker villages indicate that the Shakers initially called infirmaries "sick houses." A map of Mount Lebanon, circa 1827–39 and attributed to Isaac N. Youngs, shows small sick houses at the Church Family, the Center Family, and the Second Family. The two-story frame structures have a single entrance and either a gambrel roof, as at the Church and Second Families, or a gable roof, as at the Center Family. The presence of gambrel roofs on two of the buildings suggests that these may have been erected in the late eighteenth century. A map of Hancock drawn shortly after 1820 depicts a similar "nurse

9-1 This display cabinet, in the Church Family dwelling at Hancock, Massachusetts, contains an array of medicines, a phrenology head, and other Shaker medical artifacts.

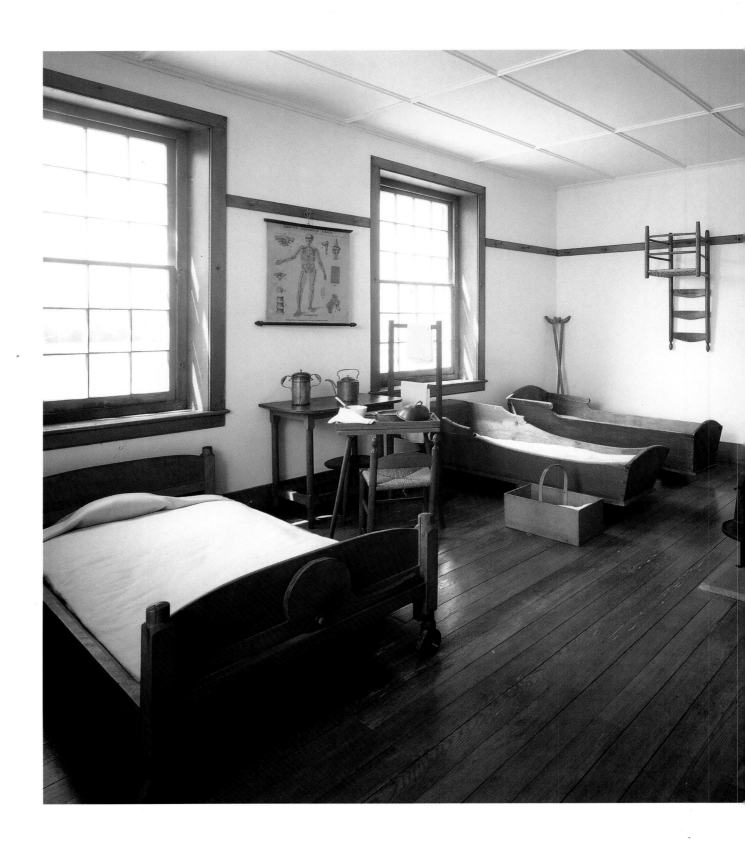

shop" standing between the Church Family's first dwelling house and the ministry shop.[32] These early infirmaries stood along the main road through the village, probably appearing much like little houses to passers-by and visitors from the outside world. One of only two infirmaries that remain standing is at Canterbury, New Hampshire. Built in 1811, the wood-frame, L-shaped building stands 2½ stories tall. Although it has a gable rather than a gambrel roof, the structure provides a good idea of the scale and appearance of early infirmaries.

The "Physicians Lot"

Brothers and sisters in the "physicians lot" tended the sick. These members lived in the sick house to provide twenty-four-hour care to those who needed it. This situation required special rules to ensure that no untoward behavior could occur, particularly since no elders or eldresses lived in the building unless they were ill. The Millennial Laws include a section entitled "Respecting Physicians or Nurses, and the Obligations of Members, thereunto," outlining conduct thus:

> 3. Brethren may not apply medical aid to sisters who are sick, without the knowledge and union of the sisters who officiate as nurses in the family. Neither should they administer any medicines to the sisters, without telling the

9-2 This exhibition room in the Hancock Church Family dwelling house recreates a sick room, complete with adult cradles used to rock and comfort the ill. Such a room would not have existed in a dwelling house, but instead would have been found in the family's infirmary.

sisters in care, what it is made of; —and sisters should do the same in these respects to the brethren.

5. If any of the brethren or sisters need assistance in the medical line, they should apply to the physicians or nurses in their own family, and of their own sex, (if there be such) and if not, to such as are appointed, and give themselves up to their direction as it respects their medical treatment.[33]

These rules acknowledge the difficulty of always having enough brothers to treat brothers and sisters to treat sisters. Thus, infirmaries are rarely found with two separate entrances. In cases of sickness, the strict rules forbidding the interaction of men and women were modified, although as the Laws indicate, interaction was carefully monitored.

Nineteenth-Century Infirmaries

In larger families, however, the Shakers attempted to maintain separation of the sexes. The wood-frame infirmary built by the Church Family at Mount Lebanon in 1858 resembles an eastern dwelling house in its size, rectangular plan, and gable roof (figure 9-3). However, it has only one front entrance door suggesting that, at least in the community of Mount Lebanon, the building had a function other than housing. The erection of an infirmary in the late 1850s was not merely a response to a still-growing population, but also to a greater demand for health care among Believers.

Treatment within Shaker communities seems to

have been better than in the outside world. Although various diseases hit villages from time to time, the Shakers' rural locations and relative isolation from the world protected them from dangerous urban epidemics such as yellow fever and cholera. Many members lived to be quite old, to their eighties and nineties. Shaker sisters no doubt survived longer on average than their worldly counterparts because their lives were not threatened by pregnancy and childbirth.

Professionalization of Shaker Health Care

As the years passed, health care in Shaker villages became professionalized. Some members were sent into the world to receive medical training. Brother Barnabas Hinckley of Mount Lebanon, who had joined the Shakers as a child, worked as the physician at the community beginning in 1837. He attended Berkshire Medical College in Pittsfield, Massachusetts, to receive his medical degree, then returned to Mount Lebanon to practice medicine. His professional training coincides with the construction of the infirmary at the village. The Church and Center Families of the community gradually increased their medicinal industry over the 1840s and 1850s. The Shakers sold many of their own products, such as veratrum viride (a tonic for heart conditions), to the world with great success (figure 9-1). Mount Lebanon had apparently committed itself to enhancing its

9-3 The Church Family at Mount Lebanon, New York, built its large infirmary in 1858, perhaps to better care for its aging population.

medical reputation both inside and outside the village by expanding the care of its own members while selling its medicines to the world.

Dentistry was also practiced in Shaker communities. Elder Henry C. Blinn of Canterbury was the most prominent practitioner. He treated members in his office in the ministry shop. His office remains more or less intact today, displaying a startling array of dental implements and an early reclining dentist's chair.

In the late nineteenth century, when a depletion of labor rendered the Shakers increasingly dependent on the services of the outside world, the villages began to bring in doctors and dentists to treat members. This corresponded to a trend in the outside world, as the science of medicine overtook traditional home remedies and people turned increasingly to trained doctors for health care. In this way, the Shakers responded to changes occurring in mainstream American society.

10 Outbuildings

The Diversity of the Shaker Landscape

FOR LACK OF A BETTER TERM, "outbuildings" will serve to encompass all the other structures at Shaker villages that do not fall under a specific building type. The diversity of Shaker life required numerous outbuildings, which provided space for specialized functions that could not be accommodated in other structures. Among these outbuildings are dairies, bath houses, privies, smokehouses, ice houses, dryhouses, and preserve houses. Because of the small size of many of these buildings and their relative insignificance compared to larger Shaker buildings, most of them have long since disappeared. However, enough have survived to indicate that each Shaker village, in addition to its grand dwellings, offices, workshops, and meeting houses, was full of various small and sometimes awkward structures.

Dairies

Each nineteenth-century Shaker family, in addition to growing much of its food, also produced most of its dairy products. In dwelling houses with large kitchen facilities, sisters sometimes made cheeses and butter right in the dwelling. However, for families with large populations, a separate dairy building was necessary to produce and store goods for the entire family. These wood-frame or brick buildings stood near the main dwelling or sisters' shop of the family, providing easy access for the "dairy sisters" and simplifying transportation of dairy products to the family dining rooms. At Hancock's Church Family the dairy and sisters' weave shop shared quarters in a 2½-story, wood-

10-1 The Sabbathday Lake, Maine, Shakers built their shingle-sided water tower in 1903. The unusual octagonal tower stands in an orchard on a hill above the dwelling house.

frame building. At Enfield, New Hampshire, the
Church Family laundry and dairy were housed in
the same 3½-story rectangular structure. At South
Union, one brick building contained both the dairy
and the smokehouse (figure 10-3).

Bath Houses and Privies

Before the installation of running water in the
dwelling houses, bath houses and privies provided
space for each family's hygiene. All these buildings
were wood-frame structures with a single entrance
and windows to let in light and air. In keeping with
Shaker laws, separate buildings existed for brothers and sisters. A bath house for the brethren still
stands at Pleasant Hill (figures 10-2 and 10-5). The
small one-story wood building, constructed in
1860, was the second such house for the brethren
of the Center Family. The ministry had separate
facilities in accordance with the precept that they
not mix with the other Shakers. The ministry's bath
house at Hancock Shaker Village is a small brick
structure with room for some wash tubs and a few
benches. A stove connected to a chimney kept the
small building warm in cold weather. A Historic
American Buildings Survey drawing of a privy at
the South Family at Mount Lebanon depicts a
15-foot-tall building with three stalls. A 2-inch-
high vent running under the eaves and two round
vents just beneath each gable in addition to three

10-2 The water house (1833) and brethren's bath house (1860)
at Pleasant Hill, Kentucky, stand back from the main road,
between the Center Family dwelling house and the East Family
brethren's shop.

10-3 In 1835 the South Union, Kentucky, Center Family built an elegant and substantial
structure to function as both their smokehouse (to the left) and dairy (to the right).

windows in the south wall provided air circulation.[34] Similar privies remain at Hancock Shaker
Village and at Pleasant Hill (figure 10-4).

Smokehouses, Dryhouses,
and Preserve Houses

Smokehouses, dryhouses, and preserve houses
were additional small structures dotting the Shaker landscape. The surviving examples of these

buildings do not seem to be distinctly Shaker, but
rather adaptations of building types present on
non-Shaker farms. Smokehouses were stone or
brick buildings used by the family to preserve
meats. As work buildings, these structures stood
back behind the main village buildings. A small
gable-roofed brick smokehouse still stands behind
the North Family's dwelling house at Whitewater,
Ohio. Dryhouses and preserve houses were sited,
like smokehouses, behind the main buildings and

10-4 This privy (ca. 1840) from Harvard, Massachusetts, now stands at Hancock, Massachusetts.

10-5 The brethren's bath house (1860) at Pleasant Hill is a small building with a gable roof. Inside, a metal tub, benches, and a stove allowed the brethren to bathe while keeping warm in the winter.

away from the street. Dryhouses, built of brick or wood, were used to dry herbs, while preserve houses, built of the same materials, provided additional space to store canned goods.

Other Outbuildings

Before refrigeration was available, ice houses stored enough ice for an entire Shaker family or village. Hancock had an ice house as early as 1844, but the one that stands at the village today was erected in 1894 (figure 10-6). In the winter Shaker brothers there cut ice from frozen lakes and hauled it to the ice house, where they stored it until the following winter. Half of the brick building's first story is lined with pine and was used as cold storage for foodstuffs. The rest of that floor and the structure's attic held ice, up to two hundred tons of ice altogether.

Other buildings served more specific functions

not necessarily required at every Shaker village. For example, Pleasant Hill built a wood-frame water house in 1833 (figures 10-2 and 10-7). Inside, a large tank held water from a nearby creek to meet the needs of the central families of the village. This building hid the ungainly form of the tank and protected the water itself from possible vandals. In addition, the brick-filled walls provided some insulation, preventing the water from freezing during the winter. The Shakers at Sabbathday Lake approached the problem of supplying water to their community in a different way. In 1903 they built their octagonal shingle-sided water tower on a hill above the Church Family dwelling, where gravity drew water down to the buildings (figure 10-1).

A wood-frame brewery (1832) once stood at Whitewater, Ohio. In the early nineteenth century

the Shakers were permitted to brew and drink their own beer, as well as to make wine and other types of alcoholic drinks. The presence of a specific structure for brewing beer was unusual, however. During Isaac N. Youngs's visit to Whitewater in 1834, he noted the structure with great interest both in his journal and in the plan he drew of the village. His map shows a large two-story frame structure with a tall smoke stack rising above the roof.[35] It is possible that the Whitewater Shakers sold some of the beer to the world as a means of supporting the community.

The fire house at Canterbury, built in 1908, demonstrates the change in architectural forms used in Shaker communities in the early twentieth century (figure 10-8). Constructed by non-Shaker builders, the fire house is a mixture of old forms and new materials. Although it is a wood-frame structure, scalloped metal siding covers the exterior, reflecting contemporary building trends in the outside world.

Although few examples of outbuildings remain, the ones that do exist help round out our notion of the appearance of nineteenth-century Shaker villages at their peak.

10-7 The water house (1833) at Pleasant Hill surrounds a wooden water tank supported on stone piers. The house helped insulate the tank, preventing the water inside from freezing in the winter.

10-6 (opposite) The Shakers erected this ice house at Hancock in 1894. Built into the side of the hill, two doors open into the building on the top level. The earth around the lower level helped keep ice and foodstuffs cool well into the summer. Double doors on each entrance also provided insulation.

10-8 In 1908 the Canterbury, New Hampshire, Shakers hired outside workers to build a fire house. The building, clad with scalloped metal siding and painted a bright red, reflected new building practices common in the outside world.

11 Burying Grounds

Reminders of Salvation

ALTHOUGH BURYING GROUNDS are not considered architecture, they are discussed here because they represent distinct physical spaces within Shaker communities. The Shakers attached considerable importance to their cemeteries. Each family kept diagrams showing where family members were laid to rest and numerous plans can still be found in Shaker manuscript collections. Many Shaker cemeteries, especially the early ones, have been obliterated since the closing and destruction of their villages. Those that survive document the different forms that the Shakers used to remember their dead.

Today, these graveyards seem peripheral, but that was not always the case. As the villages sold off land and closed the outer families, the cemeteries, usually just outside the Church or Center Family, became more isolated. Nevertheless, throughout the nineteenth century they served as constant reminders of the salvation granted to dead Shakers and the promise of future salvation for living Believers. Principal burying grounds often stood along the central road running through the community. During the peak years of a village, the cemetery would have been in or near its center. Such cemeteries can still be seen at Watervliet, New York; Hancock and Harvard, Massachusetts; Enfield and Canterbury, New Hampshire; Pleasant Hill, Kentucky; and Whitewater, Ohio (figures 11-2 and 11-3). Union Village, Ohio's main cemetery lies at the crossroads of the village opposite the site where the South Family once stood.

11-1 Standardized iron markers, such as this one at Harvard, Massachusetts, were used in the nineteenth century by most Shaker communities. In contrast to earlier markers, they recorded the names, ages, and dates of death of the Shakers buried beneath them.

The extant burying grounds provide an idea of the different types of grave markers the Shakers used over the years. Initially, dead Shakers were remembered with individual grave stones inscribed with their initials, age, and date of death (figure 11-3). Later, in the nineteenth century, names replaced initials, emphasizing a member's individual status as well as his or her place in the community, for example, Elder Giles B. Avery's stone at Watervliet, New York reads: "Eld./Giles B. Avery/D. 1890./A. 75." This type of grave marker can still be seen at Watervliet, Whitewater, and Pleasant Hill. In some cases, the Shakers moved the bodies of early leaders, including Mother Ann Lee, from graves not on Shaker property, to the villages' own burying grounds. Mother Ann's final resting place in the Watervliet Shaker cemetery is marked by a marble stone, slightly larger than the surrounding markers and carved only with her name, birthplace and date, and place and date of death (figure 1-2, page 20).

In the nineteenth century, the Shakers experimented with what they thought would be a more durable and easy-to-produce marker, an iron rod with a flat iron oval sign stamped with the Shaker's name, age, and death date (figure 11-1). The oval and rod were separate pieces, allowing mass production and standardization. These markers were

11-2 The nineteenth-century cemetery at Pleasant Hill, Kentucky, stands to the west of the present village. Individual monuments still mark some Shaker graves.

11-3 This early nineteenth-century gravestone at Whitewater, Ohio, is marked only with the initials of a Shaker. At this period, the Shakers left scant record of the individual, not even any clue as to whether the person was a brother or sister.

11-4 Most Shaker villages removed individual grave markers in the late nineteenth and early twentieth centuries to replace them with a single large stone, such as this one in the burying ground at Canterbury, New Hampshire.

approved by the Mount Lebanon ministry and used in nearly all Shaker villages. They can still be seen in the cemetery at Harvard.

The best-known Shaker marker, however, is the monolith that replaced the individual markers in the late nineteenth and early twentieth centuries (figure 11-4). These large stone monuments inscribed with the word "Shakers" stood in the center of the burying ground (now devoid of individual markers) to indicate the communal nature of the Shakers on earth and in heaven. It is interesting to note that these stones were set in place as Shaker villages began to close. The appearance and use of the stones seem to have been a matter of choice from village to village. The Hancock Shakers erected their marker, a truncated obelisk, in 1943 and included the following inscription: "In Loving Memory/of Members of the/**Shaker Church**/Who Dedicated their Lives/to God and to the Good of/Humanity/Passed to Immortality." Saved because of neglect in the early twentieth century, eighteenth and nineteenth-century markers still exist at sites such as Watervliet, Harvard, and Pleasant Hill. Fortunately, these cemeteries have survived, providing a final testament to the Shaker spirit.

12 The Legacy of Shaker Architecture

WHEREAS SHAKER COMMUNITIES throughout the United States flourished in the early nineteenth century, the latter part of that century and the first part of the next saw a drastic decline in the number of Shakers and Shaker villages. As elderly members died and young adult members departed, communities found themselves short of able-bodied workers to perform daily tasks. Left with limited resources, the Shakers began shutting down settlements.

Closing Communities

The Hancock bishopric closed Tyringham, Massachusetts, in 1875 and sent the remaining brothers and sisters to Hancock, Massachusetts,

and Enfield, Connecticut. Nearly twenty years later, in 1892, Mount Lebanon closed the Groveland, New York, community; the members there moved to Watervliet, New York. In 1899 the Shakers closed Poland Hill, one of the families at the Sabbathday Lake, Maine, community. Closings occurred in the West as well, beginning with North Union, Ohio, in 1889. In the first few decades of the twentieth century, more villages closed forever: Shirley, Massachusetts, 1908; Watervliet, Ohio, and Pleasant Hill, Kentucky, 1910; Union Village, Ohio, 1913; Whitewater, Ohio, 1916; Enfield, Connecticut, 1917; Harvard, Massachusetts, 1918; South Union, Kentucky, 1922; Enfield, New Hampshire, 1923; Alfred, Maine, 1932; and Watervliet, New York, 1938. Ever since the 1872 closing of the East Family, Mount Lebanon had been shutting down parts of its village. It finally closed in 1947. Hancock followed in 1960. With

Attic dormer, Center Family dwelling house (1824–34), Pleasant Hill, Kentucky.

the death of Sister Ethel Hudson in 1992, Canterbury, New Hampshire, ceased being a living Shaker community. Today only one community remains, that of Sabbathday Lake, Maine, with eight adult members.

The shrinking of the Shaker population at the end of the nineteenth century caused construction of new buildings to slow and gradually cease. Many structures, such as Mount Lebanon's 1875 Great House and Hancock's 1910 Barn, were built largely by hired labor. The styles of these buildings and others constructed in this period reflect more worldly designs and building techniques than did earlier Shaker structures.

Twentieth-Century Adaptations and Losses

With the sale of Shaker villages, many buildings were abandoned or demolished. Nevertheless, the communal function of Shaker architecture has persisted as former Shaker buildings and villages continue to be used by various organizations. In 1929 the Darrow School purchased many of the Church, Center, and North Family buildings at Mount Lebanon. The three remaining dwelling houses have been used as dormitories, though not in quite the same way as the Shakers used them. Mount Lebanon Shaker Village, Inc. has long-term plans to gradually buy and convert the structures to museums. However, because of lack of funding, the future of these buildings is uncertain. Stripped of their built-in furniture by a collector, the buildings have languished. Part of the site is currently a museum, but the fate of the Darrow School buildings remains to be seen. The South Family build-

ings have fared better. For many years after the Shakers sold it in 1947, the South Family property functioned as a work camp for children in the summer. The dwelling house served as the dormitory for participants in the camp. Since 1975 the buildings at the South Family have housed Sufis, members of an Islamic sect who live and work communally in the dwelling house and shops, not unlike the buildings' original occupants.

The other Shaker site still extant in New York, Watervliet, is somewhat intact. Though many Church Family buildings have been torn down, some of them remain as the Ann Lee Health-Related Facility, owned by Albany County. The South Family of the village is privately owned. Various plans have been presented in the past twenty years to make it into a community center, but nothing has happened yet.

While the Shaker museums at Hancock, Canterbury, and Pleasant Hill are well known, the fates of other Shaker villages are more obscure, though no less important. The Enfield, Connecticut, Shirley, Massachusetts, and Groveland, New York, communities are now the sites of state correctional institutions. Only a few buildings remain at Enfield, mostly barns and sheds. Shirley also has some remaining workshops and two small dwellings, once used as police barracks. At Groveland, the East Family's dwelling, kitchen, and sisters' shop remain, as do the West Family's office and sisters' shop. Most of these buildings have been substantially altered by subsequent occupants: first, by a center for the care and treatment of epileptics, and later by the New York State Department of Corrections.

The Catholic Church purchased parts of the

Attic stairs and storage built-ins, Church Family dwelling house (1830), Hancock, Massachusetts.

villages at Enfield, New Hampshire, and South Union, Kentucky. The upper Shaker village at Enfield is now the site of the La Salette Shrine, while part of the lower Shaker village is run by a separate organization called The Museum at the Lower Shaker Village. The Great Stone Dwelling, as it is known today, survives as an inn. The Catholic Church still owns the large laundry building at South Union, but most of the remaining buildings, including the brick dwelling, are open to the public as a Shaker museum.

Of the four villages in Ohio, evidence of only two remains. After the closing of Union Village, the United Methodist Church purchased much of the land. Once the largest Shaker settlement in the West, the village, known today as the Otterbein Homes, survives as a privately run retirement community. Only traces of the Shakers' huge building program remain: Marble Hall and the Center Family brick dwelling. Fortunately, Whitewater is experiencing a rebirth. The Hamilton County Park District has bought much of the land on which the

Stair rail, Church Family dwelling house (1830), Hancock, Massachusetts.

former Shaker village stood, and plans to restore many of the over twenty buildings on the property in order to open the site as a museum.

It is no accident that many of the Shaker villages continue to be used by institutions or communal groups. The rural settings of the sites are attractive because of their relative isolation and low maintenance costs. In many cases the Shaker buildings that still stand have survived because of their ability to accommodate large groups of people. Although the current uses of these sites have altered the appearance and atmosphere of the old villages, their various functions as state prisons, homes of religious groups, or retirement communities perpetuates aspects of Shaker communalism—albeit in guises their builders would probably not have sanctioned.

Shakers and Modern Design

Although the Shakers had been the object of persecution and curiosity for their religious beliefs and social practices, public interest turned to their furniture and crafts around the time of the 1876 Centennial Exposition in Philadelphia. This commemoration of the United States' first one hundred years spawned the Colonial Revival movement, which looked to the United States' early years as a source for architecture and design. This movement coincided with the American Arts and Crafts movement (ca. 1875–1920), which promoted interest in simple, handcrafted objects in response to the increasing mass-production of the industrial age. The Shakers fit the paradigms of both movements. For exponents of the Colonial Revival, the sect represented the simpler, agricultural past of colonial New England. For advocates of the Arts and Crafts movement, the Shakers represented craftspeople who produced American, hand-made, pre-industrial buildings and furniture. In both cases, Shaker-made goods fit the bill by satisfying consumers' nostalgia for a vanishing past. Brother Robert M. Wagan's exhibition of Shaker chairs in Philadelphia in 1876 may also have spread interest in their furniture to Europe, though this needs to be studied further.

The Arts and Crafts movement helped create a market for well-designed and -produced objects through its commitment to the creation of an organic art and architecture. This movement grew out of the work of England's John Ruskin and William Morris, who celebrated the rural, communal nature of artistic production. American Arts and Crafts sought traditions rooted in American history rather than relying on the traditions of other cultures. Emphasis on local or regional materials and forms also turned taste away from the ornate decoration of High Victorian style, instead employing plain forms and clean lines to express the Craftsman spirit.

Contemporary historians and consumers admired the Shakers for their simple, honest furniture. Although the Shakers had been making chairs for sale to the outside world since the late eighteenth century, they adopted some of the language of the Arts and Crafts movement in a catalog they produced to market their chairs in the 1870s. The text emphasizes the high quality of Shaker workmanship "which combines all of the advantages of durability, simplicity and lightness." Furthermore, the catalog cautions consumers "that there are now several manufacturers of chairs who have

Meeting room, meeting house (1794), Sabbathday Lake, Maine. The Shakers
added the clock to the meeting room in the nineteenth century, using it to record
the times of spirit visions and visitations during meetings.

made and introduced into the market an imitation of our own styles of chairs."[36] The copying of Shaker chairs in the 1870s attests to the great interest in Shaker crafts even at this early stage.

The Shaker aesthetic of pared-down, highly functional forms and the Shakers' perceived self-sufficiency paralleled Arts and Crafts ideals, as well as those of European movements such as the Vienna Secession, German Jugendstil, and Scandinavian National Romanticism. All these movements shared a desire to eschew academic traditions, and the belief that simplicity underlies the creation of all true art. The American design reformer, Gustav Stickley, described Craftsman architecture as "a style of building suited to the lives of people, having the best possible structural outline, the simplest form, materials that belong to the country in which the house is built and colors that please and cheer."[37]

For many twentieth-century artists and designers the Shaker style conveyed the essence of modernity. In Europe, designers like Kaare Klint of Denmark (who worked from the 1920s to 1950s) borrowed from Shaker pieces as well as from other vernacular forms to create their own functional, modern furniture.[38] Later styles of furniture and architecture, particularly the International style and Minimalism, also espoused these ideals of unornamented form. Large, open spaces filled with light, such as the interior of Hancock's round barn or the meeting room in the Center Family dwelling house at Pleasant Hill, bring to mind the work of Modernists like Le Corbusier or Mies van der Rohe. Le Corbusier's quest to create houses as "machines for living" reminds us of the Shakers' use of buildings as tools to make daily life more efficient. The Shakers' attention to details—such as door hoods or the way windows could be removed for cleaning—seems to be reflected in Mies van der Rohe's statement that "God is in the details." While it is possible that the Shakers influenced modern design as early as the 1920s, evidence of this influence before the 1980s remains to be documented.

Recent trends in furniture design point to a closer connection, however. For example, in the early 1990s Ikea, the Swedish furniture producer, mass-marketed furniture clearly inspired by Shaker design. Other companies, like Sears and Ethan Allen, have also produced their own versions of the "Shaker look," bringing the aesthetic of unadorned wood furniture into the middle-class American home.

By the twentieth century, as the remaining Shaker villages closed, people interested in the sect began acquiring the material legacy of the Shakers. The first collectors focused on Shaker manuscripts, but soon their interest turned to decorative arts. Many collectors of American antiques and folk art began scouring Shaker villages for furniture and crafts. Collectors even acquired buildings. Clara Endicott Sears moved the trustees' office from the Harvard Shaker village to her Fruitlands Museum in the town of Harvard, Massachusetts, in 1922. Electra Havemeyer Webb purchased a Shaker horse shed and moved it to her museum in Shelburne, Vermont, in 1951.

Edward Deming Andrews and his wife, Faith Andrews, became the foremost collectors of Shaker goods in the 1920s and 1930s. They subsequently published numerous works on the history of the Believers and their crafts, shaping the way the Shakers have been perceived ever since. Where-

as earlier Shaker historians had focused on the spiritual and communal aspects of the society, the Andrewses concentrated on the practical and spiritual functions of Shaker objects. They created a myth that spoke only of simplicity and perfection without pursuing the complexities of Shaker life that existed beneath the smooth, hand-rubbed surfaces of their chairs and boxes. Yet the Shakers' own intentions were to make practical furniture and buildings exemplifying and promoting the efficiency and order that they wanted in their lives, but could not always achieve.

Other projects of the 1930s also focused on documenting and collecting Shaker buildings and

East end, cow barn (1854), Enfield, New Hampshire.

decorative arts. The Index of American Design, sponsored by the National Gallery of Art in Washington, D.C., was a pioneering attempt to catalog various items characteristic of "American design." The Index included Shaker buildings, furniture, textiles, and baskets as well as examples of American folk art. The Historic American Buildings Survey, as part of the Works Progress Administration, began to document Shaker structures in photographs and measured drawings of floor plans, elevations, and details in the 1930s. The Survey has recorded many Shaker buildings that have since been destroyed.

Museums and artists also turned to the Shakers as a source of study and inspiration. Several museums, including the New York State Museum and

Fourth-floor room, Church Family dwelling house (1830), Hancock, Massachusetts.
The interior window shares light with the storage area under the eaves.

the Whitney Museum of American Art in New York City, organized shows in the 1930s that celebrated Shaker objects. The noted American artist Charles Sheeler photographed and painted many Shaker interiors and exteriors from the 1930s to 1950s, concentrating on their geometry. Sheeler and others viewed the Shakers, like the known and unknown creators of American folk art, as the epitome of American rural culture—simple, honest, and pure. Sheeler's work helped raise awareness of Shaker design, especially Shaker furniture and other movable objects.

More recently, the opening of Shaker museums has expanded awareness of the Shaker legacy, particularly architecture. The Shaker Museum in Old Chatham, New York (which opened in 1950, though not on a Shaker site) displays the best assemblage of Shaker tools and machinery. Buildings at the museum are not Shaker structures, but were adapted to resemble Shaker buildings and to house the collection. Plans to transform Hancock into a museum began before the last Shakers left the village in 1960. The museum opened in 1961 with the restoration of two buildings. Pleasant Hill, which had languished in the hands of various owners for decades, became the focus of interest among Kentucky businessmen and historians in the 1960s. Over the years, benefactors have purchased much of the land once in the hands of the Shakers and gradually restored the buildings still standing there. The site now functions as a museum and conference center.

In the past two decades Shaker decorative arts have enjoyed great popularity among a new generation of collectors, as well as a wider public. The volatile art market of the 1980s and the entry of some high-profile collectors pushed prices for Shaker objects to new highs, drawing media and public attention to the sect. This new appeal led to an exhibition at the Whitney Museum in 1986. The show, called "Shaker Design" and curated by June Sprigg, celebrated the Shaker aesthetic in much the same way the shows of the 1930s had. Chairs and tools were displayed as art, rather than as functional objects, taken out of their historic context. This presentation, though effective in focusing on the craftsmanship of the Shakers, failed to convey how the objects worked in the society's daily life or the practical reasons why they were made in the first place. The Whitney show provides evidence of the extraordinary appeal of Shaker decorative arts as modern art rather than as utilitarian historic objects.

Articles on Shaker architecture and furniture also found their way into international design magazines, such as *Domus*, *Design Quarterly*, and *Interior Design*. Through publications such as these, and more recent exhibitions, Shaker architecture and furniture has become well known outside of the United States, specifically in Europe and Japan. Since the nineteenth century, designers and collectors have seen the Shakers as representing different movements at different times: first as nostalgic reminders of the past in the Colonial Revival and Arts and Crafts movements and later as representing the essence of Modernism. At the end of the twentieth century, we continue to be intrigued by the austere elegance of Shaker furniture and architecture. The complexity of the Shakers has allowed their distinctive style to be all things to all people. We can only imagine the appeal Shaker design will have for architects and designers of the future.

Notes

1. Rufus Bishop and Seth Y. Wells, eds. "Testimonies of the Life, Character, Revelations and Doctrines of Our Ever Blessed Mother Ann Lee, and the Elders with Her; Through Whom the Word of Eternal Life was Opened in this Day of Christ's Second Appearing: Collected from Living Witnesses" (Hancock, Mass.: J. Tallcott and J. Deming, 1816), 273.

2. Joseph Meacham to Lucy Wright [1796], ms. IV:A-30, Shaker Manuscript Collection, Library of the Western Reserve Historical Society, Cleveland, Ohio (hereafter referred to as WRHS), quoted in Stephen J. Stein, *The Shaker Experience in America: A History of the United Society of Believers* (New Haven: Yale University Press, 1992), 48.

3. Stein, *Shaker Experience*, 73–76.

4. Stein, *Shaker Experience*, 73.

5. Isaac Newton Youngs, "A Concise View of the Church of God and of Christ on Earth. Having its foundation In the faith of Christ's first and Second Appearing, New Lebanon, 1856," ms. 861, Edward Deming Andrews Memorial Shaker Collection, Winterthur Museum and Library, Winterthur, Del., 502.

6. William Sims Bainbridge, "Shaker Demographics 1840–1900: An Example of the Use of U.S. Census Enumeration Schedules," *Journal for the Scientific Study of Religion* 21:4 (December 1982), 355.

7. Seth Y. Wells, "Records Kept by Order of the Church," New Lebanon, 1780–1840, ms. 7, Shaker Manuscript Collection, Rare Books and Manuscripts Division, New York Public Library, New York, N.Y., n.d., n.p.

8. "The Millennial Laws or Gospel Statutes and Ordinances adapted to the Day of Christ's Second Appearing. Given and established in the Church for the protection thereof by Father Joseph Meacham and Mother Lucy Wright The presiding Ministry and by their Successors The Ministry and Elders. Recorded at New Lebanon August 7th 1821. Revised and re-established by the Ministry and Elders Octr 1845," published in Edward Deming Andrews, *The People Called Shakers* (New York: Oxford University Press, 1953; reprint, New York: Dover Publications, 1963), 255.

9. "Millennial Laws" published in Andrews, *People Called Shakers*, 285.

10. Preface to the journal of Isaac Newton Youngs, "Tour thro the States of Ohio and Kentucky during the Summer of 1834," 25 July 1834, Shaker Collection, Emma B. King Library, Shaker Museum, Old Chatham, N.Y. (hereafter referred to as OC).

11. "Millennial Laws" published in Andrews, *People Called Shakers*, 269.

12. "Millennial Laws" published in Andrews, *People Called Shakers*, 266.

13. Giles B. Avery, "Travel Account of a trip to Enfield, New Hampshire," 1843, ms. 12744, 43, OC.

14. Brother Benjamin [Seth Youngs] to Brother Nicholas [Bennet], South Union, 26 February 1818, ms. IV:A-52, WRHS.

15. Mary Rae Chemotti, "Outside Sources for Shaker Building at Pleasant Hill," *Kentucky Review* 2:1 (1981),59.

16. "Millennial Laws" published in Andrews, *People Called Shakers*, 271–272.

17. Dale W. Covington, "Union Village and The Shaker Colonies in Georgia," Union Village Seminar (Lebanon, Ohio: Warren County Historical Society, 1989), 19.

18. Edward Deming Andrews, *The Community Industries of the Shakers* (Albany: University of the State of New York, 1933; reprint, Charlestown, Mass.: Emporium Publications, 1971), 242–243.

19. "Millennial Laws" published in Andrews, *People Called Shakers*, 285.

20. Youngs, "Tour thro the States," 3 July 1834.

21. Charles F. Priest, "The Church Family at Harvard, Massachusetts." August 1833, Geography and Map Division, Library of Congress, Washington, D.C.

22. David Austin Buckingham, "The Church Family at Watervliet, New York," March 1838,

Collections of the New York State Museum, Albany, N.Y.

23. Benson John Lossing, "The Shakers," *Harper's New Monthly Magazine*, 15 (July 1857), 164–77; reprinted in Don Gifford, ed., *An Early View of the Shakers* (Hanover, N.H.: University Press of New England, 1989), 51.

24. "South Family Journal", Mount Lebanon, N.Y., 1878–1883, ms. V:B-168, 9 December 1879, WRHS.

25. "South Family Journal", ms. V:B-168, 8 November 1881.

26. The maps drawn by Isaac Newton Youngs were copied in July 1835 by George Kendall, a Shaker at Harvard. These maps, bound in a journal, are now at the Library of Congress.

27. Edward Deming Andrews and Terry Hallock, "Shaker Church Family Washhouse and Machine Shop." HABS No. MASS-730, Historic American Buildings Survey, Prints and Photographs Division, Library of Congress, 1962 (hereafter referred to as HABS).

28. Catharine E. Beecher, *A Treatise on Domestic Economy, for the use of young ladies at home, and at school* (Boston: Marsh, Capen, Lyon, and Webb, 1841).

29. "Millennial Laws" published in Andrews, *People Called Shakers*, 276–277.

30. Youngs, "Tour thro the States," 19 June 1834.

31. Dorothy M. Filley, *Recapturing Wisdom's Valley: The Watervliet Shaker Heritage, 1775–1975* (Colonie, N.Y.: Town of Colonie and the Albany Institute of History and Art, 1975), 98.

32. Isaac Newton Youngs (attributed), "Map of New Lebanon. Columbia Co. N.Y.," ca. 1827–1839, private collection. "Hancock Church. 1820." (anonymous) after 1820, Hancock Shaker Village, Pittsfield, Mass.

33. "Millennial Laws" published in Andrews, *People Called Shakers*, 260–261.

34. "Privy (Building No. 5), South Family, Mount Lebanon, N.Y.," NY-3248, HABS.

35. George Kendall, "View of Whitewater," July 1835, after Isaac Newton Youngs, July 1834, Geography and Map Division, Library of Congress.

36. "An Illustrated Catalogue and Price-list of the Shakers' Chairs" (Mount Lebanon, N.Y., n.d.; reprint, Newton, Mass.: Emporium Publications, 1971), 1-2.

37. Gustav Stickley, *More Craftsman Homes* (New York: Craftsman Publishing Company, 1912; reprint, New York: Dover Publications, 1982), 1.

38. Renato Defusco, *Storia del design* (Bari, Italy: Laterza, 1990), 238.

Bibliography

Manuscript Collections

Edward Deming Andrews Memorial Shaker Collection. Henry Francis DuPont Winterthur Museum and Library, Winterthur, Del.

Geography and Maps Division, Library of Congress, Washington, D.C.

Historic American Buildings Survey. Plans and photographs. Prints and Photographs Division, Library of Congress, Washington, D.C.

Lossing, Benson J. Papers. Huntington Library, San Marino, Calif.

Shaker Collection. Emma B. King Library, Shaker Museum, Old Chatham, N.Y.

Shaker Collection. Hancock Shaker Village Library and Archives, Hancock Shaker Village, Pittsfield, Mass.

Shaker Collection. Manuscript Division, Library of Congress, Washington, D.C.

Shaker Collection. New York State Archives, New York State Library, Albany, N.Y.

Shaker Collection. Shaker Library, Sabbathday Lake Shaker Society, Sabbathday Lake, Maine.

Shaker Heritage Society Collection. Watervliet, N.Y.

Shaker Manuscript Collection. Rare Books and Manuscripts Division, New York Public Library, New York, N.Y.

Shaker Manuscript Collection. Library of the Western Reserve Historical Society, Cleveland, Ohio.

Published works by the Shakers

Avery, Giles B. *Autobiography of Elder Giles B. Avery.* Compiled by Anna White. East Canterbury, N.H., 1891.

——. *Sketches of Shakers and Shakerism.* Albany, N.Y.: Weed Parsons and Company, 1884.

Barker, R. Mildred. *The Sabbathday Lake Shakers: An Introduction to the Shaker Heritage.* Sabbathday Lake, Maine: The Shaker Press, 1978.

——. *Holy Land: A History of the Alfred Shakers.* Sabbathday Lake, Maine: The Shaker Press, 1983.

Bishop, Rufus and Seth Y. Wells, eds. *Testimonies of the Life, Character, Revelations and Doctrines of Our Ever Blessed Mother Ann Lee, and the Elders with Her; Through Whom the Word of Eternal Life was Opened in this Day of Christ's Second Appearing: Collected from Living Witnesses.* Hancock, Mass.: J. Tallcott and J. Deming, 1816.

The Constitution of the United Societies of Believers. 1933. Reprint. New York: AMS Press, 1978.

Dunlavy, John. *The Manifesto or a Declaration of the Doctrines and the Practice of the Church of Christ.* Pleasant Hill, Ky., 1818.

Elkins, Harvey. *Fifteen Years in the Senior Order of Shakers: A Narration of Facts Concerning That Singular People.* Hanover, N.H.: Dartmouth Press, 1853.

Evans, Frederick W. *Religious Communism: A Lecture.* London: J. Burns, 1871.

——. *Shaker Communism: Or, Tests of Divine Inspiration, the Second Christian or Gentile Pentecostal Church, as Exemplified by Seventy Communities of Shakers in America.* London: J. Burns, 1871.

——. *Shakers: A Compendium of the Origin, History, Principles, Rules and Regulations, Government, and Doctrines of the United Society of Believers in Christ's Second Appearing.* 1867. Reprint. New York: AMS Press, 1975.

——. *A Short Treatise on the Second Appearing of Christ, In and Through the Order of the Female.* Boston: Bazin and Chandler, 1853.

Green, Calvin and Seth Y. Wells. *Summary View of the Millennial Church, or United Society of Believers (commonly called Shakers) comprising the rise, progress and practical order of the society, together with the general principles* of their faith and testimony. Albany, N.Y.: Packard and Van Benthuysen, 1823.

———. *A Brief Exposition of the Established Principles and Regulations of the United Society of Believers Called Shakers*. New York: E.S. Dodge Printing Company, 1879.

Mace, Aurelia Gay. *The Aletheia: Spirit of Truth; A Series of Letters*. Farmington, Maine: Press of the Knowlton and McLeary Co., 1907.

The Manifesto. 29 vols. Mount Lebanon, N.Y., 1871-99.

Meacham, Father Joseph. *A Concise Statement of the Principles of the Only True Church According to the Gospel of the Present Appearance of Christ. As Held to and Practiced upon by the True Followers of the Living Saviour, at New-Lebanon, &c. Together with a Letter from James Whittaker, Minister of the Gospel in this Day of Christ's Second Appearance, to his Natural Relations in England*. Bennington, Vt.: Haswell and Russell, 1790.

Millennial Praises, containing a Collection of Gospel Hymns, in four parts; adopted to the Day of Christ's Second Appearing Composed for the Use of His People. Hancock, Mass.: J. Tallcott, 1813.

Supplementary Rules of the Shaker Community. Mount Lebanon, N.Y., 1894.

Wells, Seth Y. and Calvin Green, eds. *Testimonies Concerning the Character and Ministry of Mother Ann Lee and the First Witnesses of the Gospel of Christ's Second Appearing, Given by Some of the Aged Brethren and Sisters of the United Society, Including a Few Sketches of Their Own Religious Experience*. Albany, N.Y.: Packard and Van Benthuysen, 1827.

White, Anna and Leila S. Taylor. *Shakerism: Its Meaning and Message*. Columbus, Ohio: Fred J. Heer, 1904.

Wickersham, George M. *How I came to be a Shaker*. Mount Lebanon, N.Y., 1891.

Youngs, Benjamin Seth. *The Testimony of Christ's Second Appearing Containing a General Statement of All Things Pertaining to the Faith and Practice of the Church of God in this Latter-day*. Lebanon, Ohio: Press of John M'Clean, 1808.

Secondary Sources

Andrews, Edward Deming. "Communal Architecture of the Shakers." *Magazine of Art* 30 (December 1937), 710-715.

———. *The Community Industries of the Shakers*. Albany, N.Y.: State University of New York, 1933. Reprint. Charlestown, Mass.: Emporium Publications, 1971.

———. *The Furniture of Shaker Dwellings and Shops*. Pittsfield, Mass.: Berkshire Museum, 1932.

———. *The Gift to be Simple: Songs, Dances and Rituals of the American Shakers*. New York: Dover Publications, 1962.

———. *Organization of the First Communities*. Hancock, Mass.: Shaker Community, 1961.

———. *The People Called Shakers*. New York: Oxford University Press, 1953. Reprint. New York: Dover Publications, 1963.

———. "A Shaker House in Canaan, New York." *Antiques* 81 (April 1962), 408–411.

———. "The Shaker Manner of Building." *Art in America* 48:3 (Fall 1960), 38–45.

———. *A Shaker Meeting House and Its Builder*. Hancock, Mass.: Shaker Community, 1962.

———. *A Tour Through the New Lebanon Shaker Community*. 1948. Pamphlet.

Andrews, Edward Deming and Faith Andrews. *Fruits of the Shaker Tree of Life: Memoirs of Fifty Years of Collecting and Research*. Stockbridge, Mass.: Berkshire Traveller Press, 1975.

———. *Religion in Wood: A Book of Shaker Furniture*. Bloomington: Indiana University Press, 1966.

———. *Shaker Furniture: The Craftsmanship of an American Communal Sect*. New York:Dover Publications, 1964.

———. "Sheeler and the Shakers." *Art in America* 53:1 (Winter 1965), 90–95.

———. *Visions of the Heavenly Sphere: A Study in Shaker Religious Art.* Charlottesville: University Press of Virginia, 1969.

———. *Work and Worship: The Economic Order of the Shakers.* Greenwich, Conn.: New York Graphic Society, 1974.

Bainbridge, William Sims. "Shaker Demographics 1840-1900: An Example of the Use of U.S. Census Enumeration Schedules." *Journal for the Scientific Study of Religion* 21:4 (December 1982), 352–365.

Beecher, Catharine E. *A Treatise on Domestic Economy, for the use of young ladies at home, and at school.* Boston: Marsh, Capen, Lyon and Webb, 1841.

Brewer, Priscilla J. *Shaker Communities, Shaker Lives.* Hanover, N.H.: University Press of New England, 1986.

Burks, Jean. "Documenting Shaker Furniture: The Collection at Canterbury Shaker Village." Paper presented at the annual meeting of the Society of Architectural Historians, Decorative Arts Society Session, Boston, 31 March 1990.

Burress, Marjorie Burnside, ed. *Whitewater, Ohio, Village of Shakers, 1824–1916: Its History and Its People.* Cincinnati, Ohio, 1979.

Chemotti, Mary Rae. "Outside Sources for Shaker Building at Pleasant Hill." *Kentucky Review* 2:2 (1981), 49–74.

Clark, Thomas D. and F. Gerald Ham. *Pleasant Hill and Its Shakers.* Lexington, Ky.: Pleasant Hill Press, 1983.

Covington, Dale W. "Union Village and the Shaker Colonies in Georgia." Union Village Seminar. Lebanon, Ohio: Warren County Historical Society, 1989.

Crocker, Jeffrey D. *Understanding Shaker Architecture at Hancock Shaker Village: An Interpretive Guidebook.* Pittsfield, Mass.: Hancock Shaker Village, 1987.

Cummings, Abbott Lowell. *The Framed Houses of Massachusetts Bay, 1625–1725.* Cambridge: Harvard University Press, Belknap Press, 1979.

Defusco, Renato. *Storia del design.* Bari, Italy: Laterza, 1990.

Desroche, Henri. *The American Shakers: From Neo-Christianity to Presocialism.* Amherst: University of Massachusetts Press, 1971.

Dickens, Charles. *American Notes for General Circulation.* New York: Harper and Brothers, 1842.

Dormer, Peter. "Why Do the Shakers Look Like Modernists?" *Art Monthly* 101 (November 1986), 31–32.

Emerich, A.D. "American Monastic; or, The Meaning of Shaker Architecture." *Nineteenth Century* 11:3–4 (1992), 3-11.

———. "Architecture reveals visible form of inner spirit." *N.Y.-Penn. Collector* 3:3 (May 1978), 5–6.

———. "List of all extant Shaker buildings." 1965. Photocopy. Shaker Museum, Old Chatham, N.Y.

———. "The Shakers and Their Buildings." Paper presented at the regional meeting of the Society of Architectural Historians, Mount Lebanon, N.Y., 14 October 1972.

Emerich, A.D. and A.H. Benning, eds. *Community Industries of the Shakers: A New Look.* Albany, N.Y.: Shaker Heritage Society, 1983.

Emlen, Robert P. "The Great Stone Dwelling at Enfield, New Hampshire." *Old-Time New England* 69: 3–4 (Winter/Spring 1979), 69–85.

———. "Raised, Razed, and Raised Again: The Shaker Meetinghouse at Enfield, New Hampshire, 1793–1902." *Historical New Hampshire* 30: 3 (Fall 1975), 133–146.

———. *Shaker Village Views.* Hanover, N.H.: University Press of New England, 1987.

Filley, Dorothy M. *Recapturing Wisdom's Valley: The Watervliet Shaker Heritage, 1775-1975.* Colonie, N.Y.: Town of Colonie and the Albany Institute of History and Art, 1975.

Garrett, Clarke. *Spirit Possession and Popular Religion: From the Camisards to the Shakers*. Baltimore: Johns Hopkins University Press, 1987.

Gifford, Don, ed. *An Early View of the Shakers*. Hanover, N.H.: University Press of New England, 1989.

Grant, Jerry V. and Douglas R. Allen. *Shaker Furniture Makers*. Hanover, N.H.: University Press of New England, 1989.

Hopping, D.M.C. and Gerald R. Watland. "The Architecture of the Shakers." *Antiques* 72 (October 1957), 335–339.

Horgan, Edward R. *The Shaker Holy Land: A Community Portrait*. Harvard, Mass.: Harvard Common Press, 1981.

Janzen, Donald E. *The Shaker Mills on Shawnee Run: Historical Archaeology at Shakertown at Pleasant Hill*. Harrodsburg, Ky.: Pleasant Hill Press, 1981.

Johnson, Theodore E. *Hands to Work and Hearts to God: The Shaker Tradition in Maine*. Brunswick, Maine: Bowdoin College Museum of Art, 1969.

Kassay, John. *The Book of Shaker Furniture*. Amherst: University of Massachusetts Press, 1980.

Kirk, John T. "An Awareness of Perfection." *Design Quarterly* 154 (Winter 1992), 14–19.

Lassiter, William Lawrence. *Shaker Architecture*. New York: Bonanza Books, 1966.

Lossing, Benson T. "The Shakers." *Harper's New Monthly Magazine* 15 (July 1857), 164–77.

Mang, Karl and Wend Fischer, eds. *Die Shaker*. Munich: Die Neue Sammlung, 1974. Exhibition catalog.

McKinstry, E. Richard. *The Edward Deming Andrews Memorial Shaker Collection*. New York: Garland Publishing, 1987.

Meader, Robert F.W. "Reflections on Shaker Architecture." *The Shaker Quarterly* 6:2 (Summer 1966), 35-44.

Miller, Beth J. Parker. "Whitewater Architecture: A Study of Extant Shaker-Related Buildings on Whitewater-Owned Land in Southwest Ohio." Master's thesis, Wright State University, Dayton, Ohio, 1988.

Muller, Charles R. and Timothy D. Rieman. *The Shaker Chair*. Winchester, Ohio: Canal Press, 1984.

Neal, Julia. *By Their Fruits: The Story of Shakerism in South Union, Kentucky*. Chapel Hill: University of North Carolina Press, 1947.

———. The Kentucky Shakers. Lexington: University Press of Kentucky, 1982.

The New York Times. 1935-1994.

Newcomb, Rexford. *Old Kentucky Architecture*. New York: William Helburn, 1940.

Newman, Cathy. "The Shakers' Brief Eternity." *National Geographic* 176:3 (September 1989), 302–25.

Nicoletta, Julie. "Structures for Communal Life: Shaker Dwelling Houses at Mount Lebanon, New York." Ph.D. dissertation, Yale University, New Haven, Conn., 1993.

Nordhoff, Charles. *The Communistic Societies of the United States*. New York: Harper and Brothers, 1875. Reprint. New York: Dover Publications, 1966.

Nourse, Henry Stedman. *History of the Town of Harvard, Massachusetts*. Harvard, Mass.: Printed for Warren Hapgood, 1894.

Noyes, John Humphrey. *History of American Socialisms*. 1870. Reprint. New York: Hillary House Publishers, 1961.

Ott, John Harlow. *Hancock Shaker Village: A Guidebook and History*. Hancock, Mass.: Shaker Community, 1976.

Pearson, Elmer R., Julia Neal, and Walter Muir Whitehall. *The Shaker Image*. Boston: New York Graphic Society, 1974.

Phillips, Hazel Spencer. *Shaker Architecture*. Warren County, Ohio, 1971.

Pike, Kermit J. *A Guide to Shaker Manuscripts in the Library of the Western Reserve Historical Society*. Cleveland, Ohio: Western Reserve Historical Society, 1974.

Piraino-Holevoet, Elaine. "The Three Meetinghouses of the Enfield, Connecticut, Shakers." Master's thesis, University of Connecticut, Storrs, 1978.

Piwonka, Ruth and Roderic H. Blackburn. *A Visible Heritage, Columbia County, New York: A History in Art and Architecture*. Kinderhook, N.Y.: Columbia County Historical Society, 1977.

Poppeliers, John C. "Shaker Architecture and the Watervliet Shaker South Family." *New York State History* 47:1 (January 1966), 51–60.

———. ed. *Shaker Built: A Catalog of Shaker Architectural Records from the Historic American Buildings Survey*. Washington, D.C.: National Park Service, U.S. Department of the Interior, 1974.

Rosenberg, Willa S. "Shaker Buildings Preserved." *The Clarion* 13 (Spring 1988), 20.

Schiffer, Herbert F. *Shaker Architecture*. Exton, Pa.: Schiffer Publishing, 1979.

Schorsch, David A. *The Photographs of William F. Winter, Jr., 1899–1939*. New York: D.A. Schorsch, 1989.

Sprigg, June. *By Shaker Hands*. New York: Alfred A. Knopf, 1975.

———. *Shaker*. Katonah, N.Y.: Katonah Gallery, 1983. Exhibition catalog.

———. *Shaker Design*. New York: Whitney Museum of American Art, 1986. Exhibition catalog.

Starbuck, David R., ed. *Canterbury Shaker Village, An Historical Survey*. Durham: University of New Hampshire, 1981.

Starbuck, David R. "Those Ingenious Shakers!" *Archaeology* 43:4 (July/August 1990), 40–47.

Starbuck, David R. and Margaret Supplee Smith. *Historical Survey of Canterbury Shaker Village*. Boston: Boston University, 1979.

Stein, Stephen, ed. *Letters from a Young Shaker: William S. Byrd at Pleasant Hill*. Lexington: University of Kentucky Press, 1985.

———. *The Shaker Experience in America: A History of the United Society of Believers*. New Haven, Conn.: Yale University Press, 1992.

Stickley, Gustav. *More Craftsman Homes*. New York: The Craftsman Publishing Company, 1912. Reprint. New York: Dover Publications, 1982.

Swank, Scott T. and Sheryl N. Hack. "'All we do is build': Community Building at Canterbury Shaker Village, 1792–1939." *Historical New Hampshire* 48:2–3 (Summer/Fall 1993), 99-131.

Vadnais, Andrew John. "Machines Among the Shakers: The Adoption of Technology by the Mount Lebanon Community, 1790–1865." Master's thesis, University of Delaware, Newark, 1990.

Wilson, Richard Guy. "American Arts and Crafts Architecture: Radical though Dedicated to the Cause Conservative." In Wendy Kaplan, ed., *"The Art that is Life": The Arts & Crafts Movement in America, 1875–1920*. Boston: Museum of Fine Arts, 1987.

Zink, Clifford W. "Dutch Framed Houses in New York and New Jersey." *Winterthur Portfolio* 22:4 (Winter 1987), 265–294.

Index

Meeting house (1792), Canterbury, New Hampshire.

Acknowledgments

For their gracious cooperation, we thank the following institutions:

Canterbury Shaker Village
Hamilton County, Ohio, Park District
Hancock Shaker Village
Huntington Museum and Library
Mount Lebanon Shaker Village
Museum at Lower Shaker Village, Enfield, New Hampshire
Otterbein Methodist Home
Shaker Heritage Society at Watervliet, New York
Shaker Museum, Old Chatham, New York
Shaker Village of Pleasant Hill
Shakertown at South Union
United Society of Shakers

For their generous assistance, we thank:

Ginny Read & Terry Adams
Mr. & Mrs. Jim Adams
Heidi Beck
Michael Coe
Larrie Curry
Robert P. Emlen
Liz Fitzsimmons
Randy Folger
Angela Geweike
Jerry Grant
George Hersey
Tommy Hines

Cynthia Hunt
Dixie Huffman
David Revere McFadden
Robert Meader
Cheryl Robertson
Beverly Rogers
Lynn Rubenstein
Carolyn Smith
June Sprigg
Marinella Vaglio
Susan Williams
Gregory Wittkopp

For their enormous help in editing and producing this book, we thank:

Sabra Maya Feldman, Tom Stvan, Carl Taylor, John Tucker, and Helen Whybrow.

Finally, special thanks to Michael Kucher for his advice and support.

Julie Nicoletta and Bret Morgan